Faith

Two Treatises
by

Jeremiah Burroughs
1599-1646

Precious Faith

and

The Saints' Walk by Faith

Edited by Dr. Don Kistler

The Northampton Press
. . .for instruction in righteousness. . .

The Northampton Press
A Division of Don Kistler Ministries, Inc.
P.O. Box 781135, Orlando, FL 32878-1135
www.northamptonpress.org

*

Precious Faith and *The Saints' Walk by Faith* were first published in 1654. This Northampton Press edition, in which spelling, grammar, and formatting changes have been made, is © 2011 by Dr. Don Kistler. All rights reserved. Printed in the USA.

*

This book has been made possible through the generosity of Christ the Redeemer Reformed Presbyterian Church of Eureka, CA.

*

ISBN 978-0-9826155-6-0

*

Library of Congress Cataloging-in-publication Data

Burroughs, Jeremiah, 1599-1646.
 [Precious faith]
 Faith : two treatises / by Jeremiah Burroughs ; edited by Don Kistler.
   p. cm.
 ISBN 978-0-9826155-6-0 (alk. paper)
 1. Faith. I. Kistler, Don. II. Burroughs, Jeremiah, 1599-1646. Saints' walking by faith. III. Title. IV. Title: Saints' walking by faith.
 BT771.3.B87 2011
 234'.23—dc23
                    201102470

Contents

Precious Faith

To the Reader	xi
Chapter 1 　*The Meaning of the Words of the Text*	1
Chapter 2 　*Three Observations Raised and Explained*	6
Chapter 3 　*The Preciousness of Faith Discovered*	9
Chapter 4 　*Faith Is Substance and Evidence*	15
Chapter 5 　*The Application of the First Doctrine*	22
Chapter 6 　*Faith Frees the Soul from the Guilt of Sin*	26
Chapter 7 　*Faith Gives an Interest in God*	29
Chapter 8 　*Faith Puts Dignity Upon the Soul*	33

Chapter 9	37
Four Additional Reasons Why Faith Is Precious	
Chapter 10	42
Faith Enables the Soul to Do Glorious Things	
Chapter 11	48
Faith Glorifies God Most	
Chapter 12	51
Faith Puts a Believer Into a State of Happiness He Can Never Lose	
Chapter 13	53
Faith Is the Only Condition of the Second Covenant	
Chapter 14	57
Some Uses of the Doctrine	
Chapter 15	61
Directions How to Get Faith	
Chapter 16	66
Another Use of the Doctrine	
Chapter 17	68
The Second Doctrine Opened	
Chapter 18	72
The Application of the Second Doctrine	

The Saints' Walk by Faith

Chapter 1	83
The Scope and Meaning of the Words	

Chapter 2	86
The Text Opened	

Chapter 3	91
The Great Evil of Walking by Sense	

Chapter 4	97
The Saints Do Not Walk by Sense	

Chapter 5	108
An Admonition to Young Converts	

Chapter 6	111
Worldly Men Walk According to What They Apprehend to Be Reason	

Chapter 7	115
Reason Is Not That Which Should Guide a Christian	

Chapter 8	117
Reason Carries Men Upon Corrupt Principles	

Chapter 9   121
Spiritual Truths Are Above the Light of Natural Reason

Chapter 10   124
The Danger of Men Walking by Reason

Chapter 11   130
The Application of the Doctrine

Chapter 12   135
Saints Can Expect Greater Glory Than They Understand

Chapter 13   141
The Walk of a Saint on Earth Is the Walk of Faith

Chapter 14   153
The Saints In All Ages Have Walked by Faith

Chapter 15   160
The Necessity of Walking by Faith

Chapter 16   170
The Excellence of Faith

Chapter 17   179
An Exhortation to Strengthen Faith

Contents

Chapter 18   184
    Help For the Soul In Walking by Faith

Chapter 19   193
    Encouragements to the Soul In Walking by Faith

Chapter 20   206
    Motives to Draw the Heart to Believe
    In the Want of Sense

Chapter 21   222
    More Motives to Stir Up Weak Believers

Chapter 22   220
    Directions For the Exercise of Faith
    In the Want of Sense

Chapter 23   236
    Further Directions For the Exercise of Faith
    In the Want of Sense

Chapter 24   243
    Helps to Walk by Faith When God
    Appears as an Enemy to the Soul

Chapter 25   249
    Encouragement For a Saint When God
    Lets the Devil Out Upon Him

Chapter 26   257
Saints Must Walk by Faith In Times of Affliction

Chapter 27   261
More Ways Faith Helps the Soul In Times of Affliction

Chapter 28   265
Exhortation to Exercise Faith In the Evil Day

Precious Faith

A Treatise on 2 Peter 1:1:
"To them that have obtained a like precious faith"

Contents

To the Reader — xiii

Chapter 1 — 1
The Meaning of the Words of the Text

Chapter 2 — 6
Three Observations Raised and Explained

Chapter 3 — 9
The Preciousness of Faith Discovered

Chapter 4 — 15
Faith Is Substance and Evidence

Chapter 5 — 22
The Application of the First Doctrine

Chapter 6 — 26
Faith Frees the Soul from the Guilt of Sin

Chapter 7 — 29
Faith Gives an Interest in God

Chapter 8 — 33
Faith Puts Dignity Upon the Soul

Chapter 9 — 37
Four Additional Reasons Why Faith Is Precious

Chapter 10   42
Faith Enables the Soul to Do Glorious Things

Chapter 11   48
Faith Glorifies God Most

Chapter 12   51
Faith Puts a Believer Into a State of Happiness He Can Never Lose

Chapter 13   53
Faith Is the Only Condition of the Second Covenant

Chapter 14   57
Some Uses of the Doctrine

Chapter 15   61
Directions How to Get Faith

Chapter 16   66
Another Use of the Doctrine

Chapter 17   68
The Second Doctrine Opened

Chapter 18   72
The Application of the Second Doctrine

To the Reader

Never did a people live in a more reeling and staggering age, where there has been such tumbling and tossing of opinions and things, wherein there has been such strange and amazing dispensations of providences as in our days. Indeed, if you are one who walks by sight and not by faith, you shall see enough said before you every day to make a wise man mad. You shall see the earth with the inhabitants thereof like a drunken man, as the prophet describes it in Isaiah 4:20. You shall see one year men prodigally spending estates and blood to destroy that which another year with the same cost and experience they are building up. You shall see good men and good causes fare ill in the world, and wicked causes flourish and prosper in the world. And if you are not of a quick understanding in the Word and works of God, which is not to judge according to the seeing of the eyes and hearing of the ears, you would verily think by outward administrations that godliness is the thing God hates and wickedness the thing He loves.

I preface this to let you see what a necessity there is of handling such a subject this book holds forth, faith and hope standing in opposition to sense and reason being the subject matter of it. Now as the things of God are precious, so are the runnings out of the spirit of this precious man, who lives in the clear sight and full fruition of the blessedness which in the days of his abode in the flesh he so fully believed, so earnestly hoped and longed for. The intimate familiarity and converse which by the good hand of providence I had formerly with the author before his death, and more especially since his death, being the sole possessor of his papers, has given me some advantage above others in the world what works are fathered upon the author as being truly his own and what are not.

The scope of this book is to set the soul upon a sure foundation for eternity. To call off this heady, giddy age from perverse disputing to heart-searching, so that people may not take shows and shadows for real substances, thinking they stand in the faith when they daily stand strong and steadfast in their own fancies, so dropping to hell unexpectedly with false-grounded hope and security. The author saw to his grief upon what weak foundations many lay the weight of their hope for their everlasting salvation, men's understanding shining with light whose lives are as noisome as dunghills when (as they say of toads) having pearls in their heads, but their bodies full of deadly poison. He saw how a Laodicean self-conceited fullness was in his time (as it yet is) the reigning sin of our day, and a more dangerous desperate enemy to Christ and His grace than gross profaneness. I say, the author saw fearful guile lying upon men's consciences who were Protestants in doctrine, but Roman Catholics in their lives, possessed with a lazy spirit of slothfulness, self-conceited and self-flattery, and such who would rather adventure to go down to hell in a sweet dream quietly than to be inwardly touched and tried, than to set themselves upon the torturing painful rack of examination.

Therefore the reader shall find in all the works of this holy man an earnest endeavor to lay open the sound and false foundations of Christian buildings. And how sad is it to consider how men flatter themselves in their imaginary twinklings, hugging their own fancies, which may perhaps have the sense of a glow-worm, but no morning light in them. I say, how many nowadays speak and boast of high attainment of wonderful raised hopes and strong faith if we may believe them. But if you ask what did the obtaining of this hope and confidence in God cost? What prayers? What tears? What panting after holiness and communion with Christ? They can render little or no account here, only that they are full of joy, exceedingly full, rich in faith and hope, exceedingly rich, and stand in need of nothing. They are like so many who seem rich till they die, and then discover themselves worth nothing.

There is a generation of men and women who think God will provide a salvation for them as He did a wife for Adam, by casting him into a deep sleep, when he knew nothing and discerned nothing of it. They think to be carried to heaven in a golden dream, as the poet feigned of that vessel that carried Ulysses to heaven without a pilot. But, reader, here you shall find whether your hope is that heaven-born, Scripture-grounded, heart-purging, death-enduring hope, or that perishing hope of happiness (Job 8:13); a hope that shall be cast off as a spider's web (verse 14), a hope like the writing in the sand (Job 14:19), or like giving up the ghost (Job 11:20). Here you shall find whether the life you now live in the flesh is by faith in the Son of God (Galatians 2:20), or whether you live a mere life of sense, or at best a life of reason, perhaps a little refined and elevated above ordinary by natural and acquired helps, and the improvements of the common gifts and graces of the Spirit, but neither saving nor sanctifying. And because men fall into spiritual consumption quickly by too much familiarity and fellowship with sin, and for want of timely looking to get such soul-blows, such spirit-wounds when the pangs of their afterbirth comes to cost them as much and to be as bitter as those of the first birth,

I mean the new birth.

Here the saints may find proper and sovereign salves for raising up and establishing their languishing spirits, for jointing their disjointed souls and setting together their broken bones in a gospel way, not by frightening the soul to hell and swallowing it up over much grief and sorrow, and after that season is over to tell them they are too much dejected, and it's time now to begin to take heart and comfort to themselves, but by leading them to the Brazen Serpent, to the Rock that is higher than themselves, to Jesus Christ, who is able to save to the uttermost all who come to the Father in His name, seeing He ever lives to make intercession.

By setting this hope upon your consciences that they have too little exalted Christ in their hearts and too little lifted up their hearts by faith in Christ, and that as the greatest dishonor they can put upon Christ is by distrusting His promise of free grace and mercy. For the greatest honor they can put upon Him is to give glory to Him by believing. Here you shall find how faith laughs at death, sin, hell, and destruction in the face, and how it lives and looks out smilingly in the most blustering storms, deadliest confusions, and darkest midnight of desertion that can come upon the soul. You shall here learn how to kill your fears and doubts that they may never outgrow your faith any more. Here you shall find what a blind guide sense and reason is in the things of God, nay, how far short sanctified reason comes of attaining the great mysteries of salvation without the Spirit of faith and revelation in the knowledge of Christ, how reason in its primitive estate is incapable of the way of the gospel because the ground of faith is merely divine revelation.

You shall here learn—while others are poring upon and digging into the creature of satisfaction, meeting with nothing but vanity and vexation and finding coal-pits instead of goldmines—how by faith to take up and satisfy yourself in one God alone, that you may say with the Psalmist, "Whom have I in heaven but Thee? And I desire none in earth besides Thee" (Psalm 73:25), or as the Chaldee Paraphrase has it, "I have no companion on earth with Thee."

This precious faith the author speaks of will persuade you that it's not the creature, but God in it that gives comfort and content; as it is not the hot ale, but the portion that works. Faith will tell you the creature can do neither good nor hurt without God. They who live by sense upon the creature will still be chiding with the creature and vexing at it, as the people living upon Moses, eyeing him more than God, were always chiding with Moses in all disappointments. Now they who live by faith upon God, their souls will still keep silent before Him and be turning in upon Him, whether their trouble comes from sin within or sorrow without.

The soul that has once truly by faith touched Christ will be like the needle in the mariner's compass that will never stand still till it is full north. And though a jog of temptation may turn it aside sometimes from Christ its resting place, yet it still trembles and is restless till it can point itself fully towards God again, there settling and quieting itself and resting as a stone at the center. And because the ways and works of God and men are much in the dark, and no eye but the eye of faith can find out the walks of either ("I know," said a holy man, "where God treads, though He treads upon the waters, where He leaves no visible footsteps behind Him."), here therefore you shall learn how to reconcile God's words and works when promises and providences seem to cross and thwart one another.

When the soul by the eye of faith looks into the Word of God and sees what is there promised to the church and people of God, it concludes all things are well, very well, and will be so. But when it comes down from the mount, gazing and judging by sense of the works of God, it concludes all things are ill, very ill, and are likely to continue so. It is through the want or weakness of faith that we cannot put the word of promise and works of providence in a harmonious way together. When sight and sense cries out, "There is nothing but jarring and division," faith says, "Here is union and harmony." Even as discords bound with concords makes the sweetest music, they who have but little or no faith will still be reading riddles in the dark midnight of these distractions among us, while faith, plowing with the right heifer, gets into the bottom of Christ and knows all His heart and meaning in those things that stumble and amaze the world.

Let me yet add further that you shall learn how to walk by faith with an unchangeable spirit in changeable conditions. As a watch, though tossed in the pocket, yet keeps even motion, or as the cork in a net keeps it from being drawn under water by the lead, so those soul-refreshing comforts enjoyed in God will keep the head and heart above water when the soul seems to be up to the chin in misery. Faith, I say, will still keep the heart above, like the lark upon the wing singing continually, and it will keep the soul in an even temper. Being neither too much under the comforts of life, nor terrors of death, it will bring the creature in subjection to us and set ourselves and it in the proper place where both should stand. While by faith the soul keeps Christ and heaven in its heart, it has the moon under foot, and is not greatly moved at things that fall out every day, though cross to the grain of natural desires and expectations.

Faith will keep the soul clear in the midst of temptations, like the Israelites walking on dry land safely and the sea on each side, or like Peter on the waters. Faith will abase the beauty of the world without and tame lusts within. It will let us see the world is gain in the loss of it and loss in the gain of it. It will assure us that what we leave and deny for Christ we shall find in Him. Faith will wean from and moderate our affections to the world, for by uniting the soul to Christ it makes it like Him. Now Christ ruled His affections—anger, grief, joy, desire—but as the High-Priest was girt about the chest, so was Christ, and that with a golden girdle (Rev. 1:13). And so are all the saints in their measure, being baptized into the same Spirit and partakers of the divine nature. Now to be girt about the chest shows how those stirrings of our affections, all those motions, thoughts, and inclinations of our hearts, should be kept in order by the indwelling Spirit.

While men's experiences tells them every flower in the world's garden either has pricks or smells ill, and that like a dirty dog, the world besmears with fawning and that all the choicest contentment in it are mingled with much bitter, as a good day between fevers. Now faith comes in as a super addition to experience with more overpowering arguments, weaning from the breasts of creatures by holding forth a fuller breast of more satisfying good in things above.

To conclude, you shall learn how by faith to keep all your other graces alive, still active and operative, which is a blessed frame of heart. This makes the Christian indeed, when the heart of a man is heated with burning love, as well as his head enlightened with shining light. The power of godliness lies in the affections. Grace is for operation as its perfection; therefore the commands of God are for the acts, not simply for the habits. There is little to choose between having no grace and dull, sleepy habits that are inactive, I mean in regard of service and usefulness to God and man. "Stir up the gift of God that is in you," said Paul to Timothy (2 Timothy 1:6) that is, blow up that living spark within you, for so the word implies, alluding to the fire of the altar that was to be kept in and blown up continually. Christ should be in the heart of a Christian, not as a jewel in a cabinet, to be kept secret, but as a spring in a watch, to be always in motion. For want of this stirring up and acting grace continually, temptations come upon us and do what they will with us, even as standing waters stink and putrefy if they have no vent and do not run continually.

And now, reader, you see of what singular use this treatise may be to you in these heart-shaking, trembling, and patient-assaulting times wherein we live. Here is one singular use and benefit wherein this precious grace of faith helps the soul in evil times: not to be afraid of evil tidings, for faith fixing the soul upon Christ fences the heart against slavish fears (Psalm 112:7). The hour of darkness and temptation is now upon the world to try the inhabitants thereof; blessed are they who watch and keep their garments pure. Such have the promise to be kept from (or at least in, and therefore from) this hour of temptation. England this day is like the woman with the issue of blood who had spent all her living upon physicians and yet could not be healed by any. We never thought to have seen such deadly, bloody work in England so long continued; and after all that such revolutions and wheelings about, things are again into the old path.

How long shall England bleed before good blood appears? Much is already run out, and what bleeding is yet behind the Lord knows. Divine justice is thoroughly awake, yet England is not awake. How justly might the Lord say unto England, "Sleep on now; the time is at hand that you shall see what it is to play the wantons with the Word." Justly may the Lord say to magistrates and ministers, "The season is now upon you that you shall, with tears of blood, rue and lament the loss of the precious opportunities put into your hands, ways of advancing My ways, My truths, My worship in England."

Sloth, cowardice, hellish policies, and base ends shall now slay the womb that has bred all these. Righteous is the Lord in every drop of blood; we have had many alarms, many warnings, sounding in our ears many years together, yet we are not awakened nor reformed. How great is the misery upon us, and how little do we feel it? Our misery, like great blows on the head, stupefies our senses rather than begets any kindly feeling in us. Our sun may be nearer a setting than we are aware of. I mean the candlestick being removed, for it was never God's end to send His gospel to this nation and continue it so long that people should bring forth such wild grapes as England has done.

Is this commodity of so low a value that it cannot have vent in any other nation but in ours? Must this glorious gospel be laid aside as a refuse commodity in a corner, if England will not give it credit? Is the Lord so beholding to us for a dry, sapless, fruitless profession of the gospel in England? How soon may the Lord turn the key, shut up the doors and be gone, and send His gospel to a people that will bring forth better fruit than England has done? How easily can He of stones raise up children to Abraham, calling His sons from far and His daughters from the most remote corners of the earth? Who, if discerning spirits, does not see glory in great measure departed from England? Where is the Lord powerfully present in His ordinances with success and blessing as He was wont to be? How blind are our watchmen? How miserably have our leaders in church and state corrupted their way through false heartedness to Christ, taking up in the most gainful, easiest, cheapest way of religion? Going to Egypt again and turning back the people with them, saying it is best and safest to sit down by the old fleshpots? Is this the fruit of begging so long at heaven's gate, spending so much blood and laying out so many millions?

But I have already, I see, exceeded my bounds. I shall therefore now abruptly conclude, leaving the reader and this useful treatise to the blessing of the Almighty.

John Yates

1

The Meaning of the Words of the Text
"To them that have obtained like precious faith with us"
(2 Peter 1:1)

In the preface to the second epistle (which is summed up in the first two verses), three things are legible:

1. A prescription of the person saluting, by his name, Simon Peter; his condition, a servant; his office, an apostle; and his Master, Jesus Christ;

2. A description of the persons saluted: "To them that have obtained like precious faith with us"; and

3. The apostolic benediction, or salutation itself.

Those words that are usefully to be treated here are those that relate to the persons saluted, who are thus characterized by the Spirit of the Lord in this description: "To them that have obtained like precious faith with us."

This epistle was written and sent to the Jews who were converted and dispersed on the face of the earth, generally to all the converted Jews. Now (no question but) there were many of them who were rich and honorable, so that many high titles might have been attributed onto them; but the apostle gives them no other title than this: "To them that have obtained like precious faith with us."

When we write epistles, we use in the superscriptions the most respectful titles to those we write unto that they are capable of having, according to their place and trust. If we write to any who are persons of honor, we usually give them the title of honor, as the honorable ones. Yet the apostle, though he wrote to many who were rich and great too, put no other title upon them than this: "To them that have obtained like precious faith with us." He accounted this (as indeed it is) to be the most noble Christian title and badge of honor that he could crown them with: "That have obtained like precious faith with us." It is precious faith, a faith of price, and it has been obtained.

Faith is here compared to a precious stone, to a goodly pearl, and to a diamond. And so it is to them who have obtained it, to them who have had precious faith given unto them by lot (that is the meaning of the word). The word in the Greek that you have translated in your books as "obtained" signifies to have a thing by lot. So in Luke 1:9, it is said of Zacharias that he went to burn incense by lot. It was his lot to do the work. It is the same word that you have in Luke, with that of Peter, which is translated "obtained." And so I might show you in many other places in Scripture where this word is used of having a thing by lot. "To you who have obtained like precious faith," or, "to you who by lot have obtained like precious faith," that's the propriety of the word.

QUESTION. But you will say, what is the meaning of that, to have it by lot?

ANSWER. There is much in this for setting out the blessed condition of believers. There is this in it: The faith that they have, they have merely by the free grace of God, by His providence and by His work, and by no other cause whatsoever that has made any difference between them and unbelievers. As that which a man has by lot, there is little or nothing to be attributed to second causes; as in a lottery, if one has a better lot than another it is not to be attributed at all to his skill who draws it out, but merely to be attributed to the providence of God.

The Meaning of the Words of the Text

God in His free grace did so order things that this man should have a good lot, and others should not. When the Lord gave the land in Canaan to the people of Israel, He gave it, but it was by lot, to the end that they might know that if one man had a better portion than another it was only by the free grace of God. This was so that no man could boast himself of it and say, "I am better than you," or, "I am richer than you," or, "I am worthier than you." No, it was merely by God's free grace and love, and not from anything in themselves. It's as if the apostle should say, "Whereas all the world was in His presence, only God through His free grace made it your lot to have precious faith, that you should be enriched with this unspeakable gift." That this lot should be your portion and others should have their lot fall to have some part of the earth, He gives the earth to the children of men.

Take a whole congregation or town, and all of them come into the presence of God to receive their lot. God says, "I will give such a man such an estate in the world; he shall be master of a ship and shall have so much money or lands, and that shall be his lot. Another comes to have his lot and he shall have excellent parts. I will give him the tongue of the learned and so get credit that way. Another shall be born of such and such parentage; he shall spring from the loins of nobles and their blood shall run in his veins." Thus God crafts from all eternity the lots of men. Still another comes who shall not have much in this world, but he shall have faith in Jesus and he shall have heaven and eternal life; that shall be his lot, and thus God from all eternity gives every one their various lot and portion.

Your lot is to have precious faith? Oh! Your lot has fallen into good ground; you have a blessed inheritance; you were in the presence of God when there were all men before the Lord. As for unbelievers, heathens, and infidels, they were before God; it might have been their lot to have faith and you might have had what they have. But it is your lot to have precious faith and it is their lot to possess the world. This is the meaning of the word "obtained," and the elegance of the phrase is greatly darkened and eclipsed by the English word.

"Obtained like precious faith"—not only precious faith, but like precious faith. It is as if the apostle should say, "It is true, we are apostles, and we have the privilege in that we are the apostles of Jesus Christ and are called to this great office; and so Jesus Christ has graced us with gifts fit for such an office as He has called us unto. But there is not any one of you, the poorest and meanest believer that is, the weakest Christian who is a believer, who has the lowest parts of you all, but your faith is like precious with our faith. God has in this made you equal with us, though perhaps the Lord has not given unto you such gifts as to us, though you are not able to preach as we are able to preach."

It's as if the apostles should say, "You may not have the gift of miracles as we have, nor be called to such public work. Perhaps some of you are servants and young ones, but you have the like precious faith with us. We own you as brethren; we cannot look upon ourselves as at such a great distance, though you be meaner otherwise, yet in regard of faith (which is the most excellent grace of all) that you have the same with us." He does not say you have as much faith as we have. It might be that the apostles had more faith in degree than many of them, but you have the like precious faith in quality with us. It is of the same nature with ours, and by your faith you are invested with the same privileges that we are.

So the apostle would teach all such as are eminent Christians and have more grace and gifts than others, and are employed in more excellent things than others. Yet he would teach them not to despise the weakest and meanest Christians, but look upon them with high esteem, as those who have obtained like precious faith with them. It is a mighty expression that the poorest and meanest believer in the world is here ranked with the apostles. And so by the same reason may be ranked with Abraham, Isaac, and Jacob. You have the same precious faith that they had, and that all the prophets, patriarchs, apostles and martyrs had. This the apostle speaks to the encouragement of the babes in Christ who can only cry, "Abba, Father" with a spirit of faith, to those who have obtained the same precious faith with us. Thus you have the meaning of the words, and from this three precious doctrinal truths arise that will be opened in the next chapter.

2

Three Observations Raised and Explained

Here let me make three observations:
1. Faith is a most precious grace.
2. The weakest believer there is has the same precious faith as the strongest.
3. That which arises from the propriety of the words, as it is by lot. That God wholly, of His free grace, without any cause in us, has made the difference between others and us. These are the three points.

I shall principally treat here the point of precious faith, and the two following points will be interwoven in the prosecution and winding up of this most necessary and always seasonable choice truth, that faith is a most precious grace, a diamond, a jewel of great price. This same apostle, in another place of this epistle (1:7), says that the very trial of their faith is much more precious than gold. The very trial of the faith of the saints is more precious than gold. Take all the mines of gold in the earth, and for a man to have his faith tried is worth far more. Now if it is worth more to have one's faith tried than the gold of the world, how much more worth is faith itself then? If a man has gold he would give something to have it tried by the touchstone; but if it is worth something to have it tried, what is the gold worth if it proves true? Surly faith is a precious thing, that the very trial of it is more precious than gold.

Our Savior, in Matthew 23:23, speaking of the great things of the law, said in rebuking the Pharisees that they were so exact in cummin and annis, in little things; but the great things of the law, such as mercy, judgment and faith, they neglected. I think it is meant between man and man, but by way of argument we may draw a confirmation of our point in hand. If faith between man and man is one of the great things of the law, what is our faith in Jesus Christ? That is one of the great and weighty things of the gospel; faith is a most precious grace.

Now for the opening of this, it is necessary to discover a little of what faith is, and then wherein the preciousness of faith consists, and to come to the application and improvement of the point.

DOCTRINE 1. Faith is a most precious grace. But what faith? What is faith? Briefly it is this: This faith that we are here speaking of is that grace of God whereby the soul receives Jesus Christ, according as He is offered in the gospel.

Now Jesus Christ is tendered and offered as a full Savior, in whom all the grace of God is fountained up that the Lord intends to stream forth and to communicate to the children of men in order to eternal life. And Christ is rendered as one who has all the fullness of the grace of God that God purposes to give out to all of the election of grace in order to everlasting salvation. Now the soul by faith is enabled to receive and rest upon Jesus Christ alone; which grace of God, Christ lets out and bestows in the dispensation of those three offices of His—His kingly, priestly, and prophetic offices.

There Christ comes in with all the grace and goodness of God that the Lord intends for the children of men, to save them eternally. It is by faith the soul comes to apprehend this; first by being emptied of itself and taken off from resting upon any creature comforts. And being enlightened to see into the fullness and freeness of the grace of God, that He has put into His Son, it now comes and gives up itself to Jesus Christ. Faith resigns itself unto and rolls itself upon Him, and rests upon Him for all the good that God offers in Christ, so as it is willing to venture itself; to venture all the good it has and all it hopes for. It is willing to venture it all upon grace that it sees in Jesus Christ, and it satisfies itself in Christ alone. This is the nature of faith in general.

Now such grace as this is more worth than ten thousand worlds. Whenever the Lord comes to bless a soul with such grace, He gives that soul more than if He gave it the possession of all that Adam enjoyed on this side of heaven in the morning of his creation. Yes, if He made ten thousand worlds for the sake of this soul, it would not be so much as the giving of the soul this grace of faith.

3

The Preciousness of Faith Discovered

You will ask, "Wherein does the preciousness of this grace that it is worth so much appear?"

1. It is the fruit of God's election, and therefore is precious. It is the lot (as you heard in the opening words) that God in His free grace grants to these souls more than to others. And that place I suppose cannot but be known in Acts, where it is spoken of those who believed, "The Lord added to the church such as should be saved" (Acts 2:41). But in another place it is said those who were ordained to life believed; it is the fruit of God's ordination to life. In Titus 1:1 it is called "the faith of God's elect," so that it's the first discovery that God from all eternity separated this creature to do it good. What a precious thing is that! Faith is the first discovery of those eternal thoughts and counsels of love that God had for the good of such a soul, that He separated this soul for Himself to eternal life. Is not that a precious thing? I say the first discovery of those eternal counsels of God, that He had thoughts concerning your soul to do it good everlastingly. The soul that God has set apart for Himself from all eternity is in a blessed condition.

But how can it be known? Who can know whom God from all eternity, before the foundations of the earth were laid, elected to Himself? Who can know this? If any one of you could know the election of another, and the other party did not know it, you would think, if I could but go and declare to this soul that God has eternally elected him and make it sure to him, certainly I should be a most acceptable messenger of good news to him. Now faith is the first thing that God sends to proclaim what these determinations, decrees, and counsels of God were for the everlasting welfare of this soul from all eternity. God, who keeps in His own bosom, if I may so say, His eternal purposes for a long time, yet when the time comes for Him to work faith, "I will," says God, "unbosom My love to this soul and tell it what my heart has been towards him to all eternity. And I will send him a jewel whereby he shall come to understand that I from all eternity have elected him to life."

Suppose that the greatest man living should set his heart upon such a man and resolve that he will employ his power, honor, and riches to make such a man his companion; but, alas, the man is in prison all this while. Well, this great man sends him a diamond out of his own crown and sends it by his own son to this man in the prison. "Go," says he, "and carry this diamond to him and tell him that this diamond is to testify to him that I have set my heart upon him, and if I have any power, honor, or riches to make him great I will lay it out for him." Would not this be a precious diamond indeed to this man, if it should come upon such terms as these are? Yes, if it were but a little piece of silver, if it came as a token of such a thing as an earnest penny, it would be worth more than thousands of pounds.

Certainly wherever God savingly works faith in the soul and sends to this soul, and that by the Spirit of His own Son, He sends it as a testimony to him that He has set His heart upon such a soul and intends forever to do him good. Whenever God wrought faith in your soul, He did as much as if He should say to you, "Here, take this grace for a certain argument that I have set and fixed my heart upon you from all eternity. And if I have any power and mercy, if I have any happiness in Myself to make you happy, you shall be a happy creature forever. Take this grace for a testimony of it and make much of it." Now is not this precious? What is this worth that comes thus unto a soul? All that you have known experimentally, what the work of faith has meant in your souls, take it thus as a sure pledge of God's infinite eternal love.

Every time you meditate and think on the way of God's working this grace in your hearts, be raised in your thoughts to prize and esteem it as that which has come from God as the fruit of His eternal election. It is the faith of God's elect. God may give unto a man riches, ships, good voyages, and kingdoms, and this may be no argument of His eternal love. If He should give him kingdoms, what is that? He might give a man or woman to be king or queen of all the world, and yet such a one may be the object of His eternal hatred for all that, a vile person and the basest of men. Therefore there is not so much preciousness in all these things. But when the Lord gives faith, this is the evidence of eternal love.

2. As for the work of it, faith is the first grace that cries (if I may so say), "Land!" when the soul is in the tempest and storm of a troubled conscience. It is the first grace that cries, "Land," in time of whatever extremity the soul is in—and therein exists the preciousness of it. The soul that understands its own misery, the danger that it is in, the wrath of God that hangs over it, and then has trouble of conscience, is as a man in the midst of a storm and tempest at sea, and ready to be swallowed up in the waves of woeful trouble of conscience. It is faith that gets up upon top of the mast and cries, "Oh! Be of good comfort. I see

land. I see such a place." Oh! You account that more to you than if you had never so much money given you at that time.

This is the work of faith when the soul is in the midst of affliction and troubles, and waves of a troubled conscience tossing it up and down, that it apprehends itself ready to be swallowed up in the gulf of eternal despair. The soul sees itself ready to be plunged into and swallowed up of the bottomless gulf of eternal misery. At that very time faith is the grace that gets up upon the mast, gets up some promise or other and cries to the soul, "I see land. I see hope of mercy, hope of help, though my condition is a miserable one, though I apprehend a most dreadful breach between God and my soul. I have apprehended God as an eternal enemy unto me, and have been afraid that I should have been the soul that should have lain under the eternal curse of an infinite God, and have been fuel for His provoked wrath to all eternity. But, blessed be God, I see land. I see a way of help for such a soul as I am." Oh! How precious is this faith that enables the soul to see hope in the time of the greatest extremities of all. God gives this grace to the soul to discover hope when the heart is ever so low and ready to be overwhelmed.

3. Faith is a most precious grace in that it has the most excellent and glorious objects that can be. It is the preciousness of the objects of faith that shows the preciousness of this grace. What is the object of faith? God Himself, nay, in a particular manner, God reconciled. It is God in Christ. It is God manifesting Himself in His Son, and so God comes to be a most glorious object unto the soul than God taken merely as He is in Himself, the First-being of all things. And unless God was an object of faith, first,

The Preciousness of Faith Discovered

He could not be an object to the exercise of any other grace but in a natural way.

Consider this, if there is not faith to make God to be the object of the soul, and the soul loved God or feared God, how does the soul love God if first faith has not presented God in this manner? Only as the First-being and as the Fountain of all good, and fears God as the great and mighty God of all the world. But now faith presents God to the soul as an object in a higher way than otherwise He could be. And it is faith that forms the object for all other evangelical graces. Faith is exercised upon God in a way of a mystery, not in a natural way. The object of faith is the Son of God, the Second Person in the Trinity, God-man, God reconciling the world to Himself. All mysteries of the gospel are the objects of faith, and the glorious counsels of God about man's eternal estate are the objects of faith, such things as eye has never seen, nor ear heard, neither can enter into the heart of man; that is but a mere man who has but a natural ability to perceive. These are the things that are the objects of faith. Indeed, till faith comes in to the soul and presents these glorious objects that are the most immediate objects of itself, presents them for other graces to work upon, till that time those that we call graces of love and fear and humility and all those did but work in a natural way before.

There was a kind of love and fear and humility before, but what makes the difference between that love that is but a common grace or humility, that is but a common grace; for there is a kind of love and fear of God and humility just like unto the true saving grace of God. I say there is a like to them; yet they are common graces and common gifts. Now here lies the difference: Before these graces (so we may call them, though but common) they acted upon God in a natural way; but now faith presents God and the mysteries of the gospel in a supernatural way, in a mysterious way to the soul, so that that love which was acted upon God but merely as He was the First-Being of all things in a natural way, now it acts upon God as the Father of our Lord Jesus Christ. Before the soul feared God, but only as a great God and one who is infinitely above him. Now the soul fears God as He reveals those glorious things in His Son. The soul fears God as a Father, with a filial fear, as being reconciled to Him in His Son. So faith, then, is a precious grace because the objects of it are so precious; and it is that that presents the objects of all other graces to them in a supernatural way. Indeed, faith makes their objects to be supernatural to them, therefore a most precious grace is this grace of faith.

4
Faith Is Substance and Evidence

Faith is precious because it gives a substance to things hoped for, and an evidence of things not seen. The grace of faith is a most precious grace because it is that which gives substance unto things hoped for, and an evidence to the things that are not seen. In Hebrews 11:1 there is such a description of faith as we do not have in all the Book of God besides: "Now faith is the substance of things hoped for, and the evidence of things not seen."

I wish here to open this a little, that we may see what abundance of excellence and preciousness there is in faith. It is the substance; the word in Greek is that which gives a real substantial being to it (things that are hoped for). Things that have no reality of being in themselves for the present, faith makes them real and present to the soul; that is the meaning of this first expression, "the substance of things hoped for." Those things that otherwise might seem to be but notions, or imaginations and fancies, and the conceits of men, faith makes them to be the great realities in the world. Faith give them a substance, makes them all substantial things.

Many of you, it may be, have heard much of the kingdom of heaven, of the glory of the soul that is departed, and what body and soul you shall have hereafter with God in heaven, the vision of God and the presence of God and the like. But now if this grace of faith is not in the soul these things are but merely fictions of men, and I fear lest they have been so to many mere imaginations. These are fine things that the minister speaks of, witty notions and curious fancies of men, and such kind of thoughts I fear many have of them.

Certainly all carnal hearts are possessed with such kind of thoughts of the kingdom of heaven. "Why do you tell you me of such things? Give me house and land, and let me enjoy my estate here in the world, for these other things are such as are above us." Such kinds of reasonings are the whisperings of some men's spirits.

Oh, the poor thoughts men have of the things of the kingdom of heaven before faith comes into the soul. But when faith comes into the soul they are made the most real things of any in the world. The soul comes now to see those blessed and glorious things that are revealed in Christ about the kingdom of heaven, the most real and substantial of any things in the world, and now is ashamed of those vain conceits that it had of those things heretofore. And indeed, the things of the world are but fancies in the hearts of believers.

Here is the change that faith makes: Before faith came the things of the world were substantial, and the things of heaven were imaginations and fancies. But now when faith comes, the things of the world are but fancies, and the things of heaven are the substantial things. Thus the Scripture speaks of the things of the world, that they are but much fancy. It is said of Agrippa that he came with much fancy. But as for the things of heaven and eternal life, they have a substance in them, a reality in them. As the apostle says, "Faith is the substance of things hoped for"; it realizes them to the soul.

Further, faith is the substance of things hoped for. Though the things are not in possession for the present, yet it gives a substance to them. For example, for you to be in heaven and enjoy the presence of God, you are not now actually in heaven, but faith makes it as if it were actually done; it makes those things to have a substance (as the word may be translated). It gives the things of heaven a present substance to your soul. Sometimes Scripture speaks of the kingdom of heaven as that which is in you. It was a speech of Ecolampadius when he lay upon his sick bed, and they had him think of heaven, "Why, I bless God I am in heaven."

Consider as it is with despair (the opposite of faith); it makes hell as present to the souls that despair. One who is in despair feels the very wrath of God presently burning upon him; he not only fears that he shall go to hell afterwards, but even feels himself in hell already. It was Spira who said, "Verily, desperation is hell itself." And many poor people who have lain upon their sickbeds, wicked and ungodly men and women who have had horror upon their consciences, have cried out that they have been in hell already.

Now as despair on the one side, which is contrary to faith, has the power to make hell torments to be real and present to the soul, so faith on the other side, being contrary to it, has that virtue and efficacy in it to make all the glory and blessedness of heaven to be real and substantial to the soul.

I shall proceed to the second branch of this description: Faith is the evidence of things not seen.

OBJECTION. But are these things real?

ANSWER. Yes, faith gives the evidence.

OBJECTION. But they are not seen; if heaven were as open to men as it was to Stephen, and I could see Christ at the right hand of the Father as he did, then it would be something.

ANSWER. The text says faith is the evidence of things not seen. It is the demonstration. The word that is translated in your books as "evidence" is the word that signifies to demonstrate and convince by the strongest arguments that may be. Faith convinces by argument and makes things clear and evident to the soul. It is faith that gives such a piercing eye that the soul is able to look up to heaven to the throne of God and see Jesus Christ sitting at the right hand of the Father, making intercession for the soul, to see it as really as if he should see one at the right hand of the judge presenting a petition; for certainly faith has as piercing an eye as Stephen's bodily eye had. But certainly faith (that is the eye of the soul) is capable of a higher elevation than the eye of the body possibly can be.

The bodily eye is precious, that crystal pearl that is in a man's eye. What man in the world would give but one of his eyes for any diamond or pearl upon earth? It would be an unworthy thing for any to make such an exchange, to give both his eyes to lose the benefit of those things he sees in nature, of the sun, moon, and stars, or of the seas. What man in the world would lose such a benefit? Certainly there is no man who would have lost the benefit of that he has seen, and of his present seeing for a whole world (if he were a wise man). Now if God has placed such a thing on one's body, that shall be of such great use to discover such great things of God unto us as our eyes do, for by our eyes we come to see the wonderful works of God, and much of God comes to be let into the soul by the eye. You who have been abroad and seen the wonderful works of God, oh, how much of God has been let in, especially if you have had gracious hearts, you might have had abundance of God let into your soul by that which you have seen with your bodily eyes.

Faith Is Substance and Evidence

But now argue a little from the less to the greater. If such a bodily thing as a man's eye has so much excellence and preciousness in it, and lets in so much of God to the soul, oh, what is this diamond that God puts into the soul! How much does that let in of God to the soul! Then a man comes to see the wonders of God's law and gospel, when God gives him the eye of faith. And there is the like difference between a man who does not have faith and another who does. It is the same difference as if a man was born blind, or were shut up in a dungeon, and suddenly this man's eyes should be opened and he should come and see all the great things of God in the world. This man would behold the glory of the sun. He had heard talk of the shining of the sun and of the heavens, and of the stars and moon and seas and trees and fields and beautiful things in the world, but, alas, he did not know what they meant. He only heard people speak of them. Perhaps he could talk of what he heard before; but now his eyes are opened and he comes to behold all these things.

This is the kind of change there is in the hearts of men when God puts faith into them. They come to have another eye to let in the great things of Christ, and to see them evidently, such evidence that the soul is content to venture all that it has upon it. Such evidence one has who has faith. However other men will not venture anything for the things of eternal life that they hear preached unto them. They will not venture the parting with any one lust. They will not venture the loss of their estates if they have but hope of gaining never so little a matter by any sinful way. They will not venture the loss of their sinful gain because they look not upon these things as real.

But when God puts faith into the soul, the soul says, "Take all. I am content to venture my estates, my name, my liberty, all my comforts; content to venture my soul; content to venture eternity upon this word of God that reveals such things as these are."

Here is faith at work, and by it you may see that Christians who are never so poor and weak, yet they have such faith with those who are most eminent. Whereas there are some who have excellent parts, learned doctors that can talk more of faith and religion, but they, not having faith to make the evidence to their souls, will venture nothing. Yet you shall have a poor man or woman who works at their day's labor for their daily bread, to whom God has given faith, they will venture more for God and Jesus Christ than your great doctors.

Here is the preciousness of faith: It is the substance of things hoped for, and the evidence of things not seen. There are many things of God that we have made known by reason; faith elevates reason and discovers those things more gloriously to us than reason could do. Therefore the apostle, in speaking of the excellence of faith, says in Hebrews 3:11: "Through faith we understand that the worlds were framed." Why, do we not understand that without faith? A man by the light of nature can know that nothing can be eternal of itself. Ah, but, says the apostle, by faith we know that the worlds were made. It's as if he should say, "Indeed, there are many things that you know by the eye of reason; but when you come to have faith, you shall know in a higher manner than ever you knew before.

Faith will give a new light to all things. All things will become new; there will be a new world. As the difference between the light that there is in heaven (the place of the blessed) and the light that is here in the world, certainly it is different. Now we have the light of the world by the sun, but in the highest heavens, there is no sun there and yet there is light. As much light as we have here, and more too, the blessed saints in heaven have light, and yet they have not the light of the sun there.

Now there is a great deal of difference between that light and the light of the sun. For example, in the night season you have a candle, and you have light then; but there is a great deal of difference between the light of the candle and the light of the sun. So there is a great difference between the light of the sun and the light of God in the highest heavens. There is as much difference between the light a man has to understand things by reason and of his understanding things by faith. He understands that the same things as I can see by light of a candle. I can see the same things by the light of the sun; so when I come to heaven, I may see the same things that I see in the world as the bodies of the saints see, but with another light, the presence of God enlightens the place. So faith is like that light that is in heaven, the place of the blessed that discovers things by the presence of God, it is indeed the radiation of the presence of God to the soul.

It was a speech of Luther's, "Faith is a certain beam of the very divinity that is shed down into the heart of a believer, a beam of the divinity, that as God in heaven by His own presence filling that place with the beams of his own light." So God comes to the soul and fills the soul with His presence by working faith in it, and so makes it full of light. It is a kind of omnipotent thing and the virtue of it is inestimable and infinite. So said Luther (a man who was acquainted as much with the excellence of faith as any man that I know of since the apostles' time). Thus it is evident what a precious thing faith is. The application of the point follows.

5

The Application of the First Doctrine

By that which has already been said about faith, it is enough to make many people to be somewhat suspicious whether their faith is of the right stamp and complexion or not. Faith is a most precious grace, and you have heard how precious it is in many particulars. Many may go away and think with themselves, "Lord, how far is this from my faith?" It's true that some faith is higher than others; but the weakest faith in the world is equally precious. It's of the same nature, though not altogether so glorious. Faith is this precious stone, and the difference between this faith and the faith of the most people in the world is as between the precious diamond and the common pebble stone that lies in the streets.

You who are mariners, you see what an abundance of little stones there are with fine streaks and curious colors that lie upon the seashore sometimes among the shells. Well, it may be that if children should come and see such pretty colored smooth stones they would be pleased with them; but now a wise man would think these were but common stones. And if you should laid your ships home with such stones as these, what freight would you make? You would lose your entire voyage and be but laughed at for your pains.

The truth is, the faith that the soul must have is a diamond, but the faith of most people in the world is but like the glittering pebble stones. Perhaps you have many common gifts and you think that these are the fruits of your faith, and so think that your stone is right

The Application of the First Doctrine

because of your common gifts. But when the Lord, that great Lapidary who shall try stones, shall come and try it, He will find your supposed diamond to be but a bristol-stone, a piece of rock quartz, just like the stones that children will take to be diamonds, but they are soft; they do not have the hardness that a diamond has, and will not endure what a diamond will.

Just so I say it is for a man who shall be persuaded that he has got a diamond and thinks he is enriched by it, but when it comes to be examined by the skillful jeweller he says, "I will not give you two pence for it." Oh, how that man will be cast down in spirit! Oh, what dejection will there be in the hearts of men and women hereafter who think they have faith. If your faith proves to be this precious faith you are a blessed creature forever, whatever you lack in this world. But if upon examination your faith proves to be as a bristol-stone, proves to be too soft, it would be worth nothing at all. It's not enough for a man to say, "Well, suppose my stone is not a diamond, yet it is somewhat near one; and therefore I hope I may have half the price of a diamond." No, either it must be a right diamond or else it is not worth more than an ordinary common stone.

So though your faith should come to be never so near the true faith, never so like it, if it should come so near it as to prove to be the faith of miracles, at the day of judgement it would not be worth two pence to you. Oh, therefore you need to look at this precious faith so that you do not content yourselves with the common faith of the world that you find in every highway. For a man to have faith by which he can swear, it is a sign he does not account it precious, that he will pawn it upon every action. If a man had a diamond worth ten thousand pounds, would he pawn it upon every trifle, upon every word? You do not know the worth of your faith.

I shall lay down this one thing for a note to try whether your faith is true or not: The faith that is this precious faith, God in some measure makes the soul to have a right knowledge of it (I mean the soul that thinks it has faith—it's true some may have it and not know it). But if a man or woman says, "I hope I have this precious faith," if you can say you hope you have it, then certainly this will be. You cannot but esteem of this more than if God had given you more than ten thousand worlds for your portion. Oh, then you see the infinite riches of the grace of God towards your soul in this; then God has taught you to admire His infinite goodness to you, that He should give you this infinitely precious grace of faith.

God does not give faith as if a man should give a diamond into the hands of a fool or a child. If a man gives a diamond, he will say, "Now look at it; here's a diamond that you may make yourself a rich man forever, and therefore look to it that you may improve it." So whenever God gives this precious faith to the soul, He gives it so that when once it is discovered to the soul, for all the while it is not discovered, there God's hand is upon it, and keeps it safe that the soul shall not lose it. For when God's hand comes to discover it to the soul, He says, "See, here is that which you must live upon; here is that which must bring you to eternal life if ever you are to be saved." And the soul that hopes it has faith stands and admires God's infinite goodness for that grace of His.

Now I'll appeal to you but in this one note. You who hope that you shall be saved by faith, when was your heart taken with this excellence in the grace of faith? When were you in your closets in secret blessing

God for this, and wondering at God's goodness because of this? Adoring and magnifying, worshipping, and praising the great name of God that He has bestowed such a rich jewel upon you, that you must profess to the glory of His name is more to you than if He had given you all that ever He created to possess—if you have done this, it is a good argument that the soul that is so afflicted with the grace of faith, though it is weak faith, yet it is that precious faith that is here spoken of in the text.

6
Faith Frees the Soul From the Guilt of Sin

Faith is a precious grace because it is that grace that frees the soul from the guilt of sin. That great encomium commendation that we have of faith so often in Scripture, that we are justified by faith, sets out the preciousness of grace. It is that grace that delivers the soul from the guilt of sin, and no other grace but that does. Other graces may be signs that a man's being is delivered from the guilt of sin, but there is no grace by which we are delivered from the guilt of sin but by faith. A man indeed cannot be delivered from the guilt of sin without repentance; he must repent, but it is not repentance that frees him from the guilt of his sins. All the repentance in the world will not do it unless faith comes, so that though without other graces we cannot be freed from the guilt of sin, yet faith is the thing that does it. It is not only a grace without which we cannot be freed, but it is that grace by which we come to be freed. We are justified by faith, says Scripture. It never says we are justified by love, but by faith. All means under heaven cannot do it; the soul has to deal with Christ in point of justification only by his faith.

Luther has an expression: "In the point of justification, there Christ and faith are all alone, as the bridegroom and the bride in the bedchamber are alone. When they come abroad, then they have their train and friends go along with them, but they are alone in the bedchamber. So in our conversation, in the course of our lives, there we have the train of all other graces; but the point of justification is as the bedchamber, and there only Christ and faith, and nothing else is to be. If you bring any thing else to join with your faith in the point of justification, you spoil all."

There may be much means for the soul to obtain pardon of sin, hearing the Word, many duties being performed; all this does not free the soul from guilt. Yea, there may be many prayers made and cries to God for mercy, perhaps many tears shed, much sorrow, much trouble, but this does not do it. That which cannot be done by all duties, by all tears shed, by any repentance, by what help men or angels can afford, this is done by faith, and therefore faith is a most precious grace.

Many a soul has been a long time under the sense of sin (the spirit of bondage), has been seeking for the pardon of sin, and would give all the world and the things therein, if they had them, for the obtaining of the pardon of sin, and deliverance of their souls from those chains of guiltiness that are upon them. Now when God sends faith into the soul, the work is presently done, at an instant, in the twinkling of an eye; that which other means have been diligently and laboriously used for many years and could not do, that faith (when it comes into the soul) does in a moment. A sinner that has been guilty of the greatest, of the vilest, of the most notorious, abominable sins in the world, if God comes but once to send faith, this precious grace, into that soul, such a soul is immediately as clear from sin as a child new born (I mean from the guilt of it)—yea, and a great deal clearer too!

The first instant that faith is in the soul, such a sinner, who was too vile before, is as clear from the guilt of sin as ever Abraham, Isaac or Jacob was, as any of the prophets and apostles, yea, as clear of it as the saints are in heaven! Oh, what a precious grace is this grace of faith, that shall make such a mighty change and alteration, that one who before had such a load upon him, and such woeful guiltiness, did apprehend itself to have even the chains of darkness upon it, being held by the cords of its own sin, and being bound over to eternal death, comes now in one instant to be free from all everlastingly, so as it shall never return again upon him. This is the work of faith in justifying a sinner. And it not only frees you from the guilt of your sin, but puts upon you an everlasting righteousness. It clothes you with the white robe of the righteousness of Jesus Christ, so that you stand now before God (all the guilt of your sin removed) in the clothes of your elder brother Jesus Christ. By this we are looked upon as righteous in and through Him, the Lord our Righteousness. Oh, precious is the grace of faith!

7

Faith Gives an Interest in God

Faith is precious because it gives an interest in God, in Christ, in the promises, and in heaven itself.

It gives the soul, I say, an interest, not only frees from the guilt of sin, but gives the soul an interest in God. It makes the infinite, eternal First Being of all things, the Fountain of all good, to be its portion. Such a soul can say, "My God and my Lord," by a spirit of faith, which is a spirit application.

Faith is not only a discovering grace, as was opened, not only the critical eye that lets into the soul glorious objects, but an applying grace, an appropriating grace, and a uniting grace. It is that which gives you a right to all the attributes of God. If there is anything in God that can make you rich, that can make you happy, faith gives you a right to it; it's your own. By faith you who were before without God in the world, had no right at all unto Him, but indeed were an enemy to Him, now you come to have a right to all that there is in God. All His power, wisdom, mercy, and His faithfulness, His holiness and goodness, are all yours. There is an infinite excellence in this that I am speaking of; but I must not stand to enlarge everything here, for it must be a very large subject to show what are all the benefits we have by faith. It shall be sufficient to name them together, to show the lustre and excellence of this grace of faith.

So you have an interest in Christ. Christ is yours. That Christ, whom God the Father is infinitely satisfied in, is made yours. If there is anything in Christ that can do you good, anything that Jesus Christ has purchased that can make you happy, it is your own; you may claim it as your own, as you are made one with Christ. Here is the difference between faith and other graces: Other graces make the soul to be like Jesus Christ, but faith makes the soul to be one with Jesus Christ—and there's a great deal of difference between those two, to be like another thing and for it to be one with it yourself.

Your patience, your humanity, your heavenly-mindedness makes you like Jesus Christ; but your faith makes you to be one with Jesus Christ, to be a member of His body, to be one as the husband and the wife is one, to be one as the branch and the roots of the vine are one. Nay, one nearer than that, for the Scripture says of believers that Christ is in them and they are in Christ. Now it is not so with the branches of the vine and the roots; though the branches are of the root, yet the branches are not in the root. But believers are in Christ, and Christ is in them; you are made one with Jesus Christ, and this oneness will appear hereafter. "Father, I will," said Christ, "that those that Thou hast given Me may be one with Thee, as Thou and I art one." By being one with the Son you come to be one with the Father, and this is the preciousness of faith.

Besides, it gives you an interest in all the precious promises; and therefore faith is more precious. As for that I shall not need to go far from the words of my text. Read the fourth verse of this chapter: "Whereby are given unto us exceeding great and precious promises, that by these you might be partakers of the divine nature." Here are precious promises by which we come to be partakers of the divine nature. Certainly that grace which gives us an interest in precious promises, by which we become partakers of the divine nature, must surely be a precious grace.

You account highly such a voyage or such a ship, a rich ship, that brings in great riches from the East Indies. You say, "Here a ship has come that is worth so many thousands pounds." The ship is not worth so much, but you account the ship to be so rich. Why? Because it brings in such rich commodities as it does from those parts. So if a ship may be called rich because it brings in such rich commodities, then surely faith may well be called precious that brings in all the precious and rich promises that are more worth than all the riches of both Indies, yea, all the world.

That which gives the soul interest in so many promises must surely be precious. If you should have an interest given to you in leases and bonds and bills worth many thousands of pounds, you would account them to be precious that should interest you in such bonds, bills, and leases. Now all the promises of the gospel are so many bonds, bills, leases, and conveyances from God to the soul; and it is faith that brings in all these and makes all these to be yours. Certainly you might read of precious promises in the gospel, but what have you to do with them? They are none of yours without faith. But immediately, upon faith coming into the soul, all these promises are made yours; all those precious things in the gospel are made immediately over to you. Now you may read over the Book of God and find precious promises that were made to any of the saints of God heretofore, and you may say and plead in Christ's name, "This is mine."

Men who are carried on by presumption may think they have an interest in God, in Christ and the promises, but this is merely a delusion. I remember reading of a madman in Athens who would run to the shore and cry of every ship that came in "This is mine, this is mine, this is mine," and would have a book to write them down, and verily would be persuaded that all was his. But afterwards, when he came to his senses again, he was troubled that he had lost so much pleasure and delight.

Many who by presumption are persuaded that they have interest in all the excellent things of God, and of Christ in the Word, it proves to be but a mere fancy. But faith indeed gives a real interest in all those things, so that when you read over the Word of God, when you read anything about the excellence of God, you can claim that this God is your God. And when you read anything about Jesus Christ, any of His excellencies, you can say, "He is my Savior." And, further, when you read anything in any of the promises, you may claim it as your inheritance; so heaven is as really yours as anything you have in your house is yours, and a great deal more real and certain. Holiness indeed may bring you to a possession of heaven, but faith is that which gives you interest and title to it. One thing may give you title to such a piece of land, but something else must give you possession. Faith gives you interest and title to heaven, but holiness brings you to it; for without holiness, no man can see God.

8
Faith Puts Dignity Upon the Soul

<u>Faith is precious in regard of the dignities it puts upon the soul. It makes a man the son of God. It makes a man heir of the world. It not only makes a man an heir, but a co-heir with Christ. It makes him a free man of the New Jerusalem.</u>

The glorious dignities that faith puts upon the soul prove the preciousness of faith. Why? What does it put upon the soul? It puts this dignity, to many as received Him, said John, "He gave power to become the sons of God" (John 1). That which is translated in your books as "power" loses its elegance in the English; it is an authority to be the children of God. They have such power as has a kind of authority with it; they have authority to be called the children of God. They can claim this: It is their right to be the sons of God, even to them that believe on His Name, the text says.

Other men call God Father, but they do not have the right and authority to do it. By what warrant do you do it? But now when you have faith, by warrant you may call God Father, you come to be made the children of the living God whereas before you were a child of the devil. But now you are a child of the living God, sons and daughters of God, able to sit at the table of God as His children, and His heart is towards you as towards children. You are of God's household, among His children. When you have faith you come to have dignity, for so we are the children of God by faith. He puts it upon faith in the Epistle to the Galatians rather than upon anything else.

By this we come to be heirs, heirs of all the world. As soon as a believer has faith, though never so mean and poor in the world, yet, I say, he comes to be an heir of all the world. You have such an expression respecting Abraham in Romans 4:13: For the promise that he should be the heir of all the world was not to Abraham or to his seed through the Law, but through the righteousness of faith. The promise that he should be the heir of the world, how was it not through the righteousness of the Law, but through the righteousness of faith? It was through that that Abraham had the promise of being heir of the world.

Now by faith we come to be of the seed of Abraham, and you know the children inherit the father's estate when he dies. And it is not with Abraham's children as it is with others who have the eldest to be the heirs, but every one of Abraham's children inherits the blessing of Abraham. Look what was the real blessing of Abraham, and that is the blessing of every child of Abraham. So as Abraham by faith was made the heir of the world, then certainly every believer that is a child of Abraham is an heir of the world.

You will say that "believers are the heirs of heaven." This indeed we all grant, and say that they shall go to heaven, and are heirs of heaven. But that they should be heirs of the world, it may be that you have not thought so much of. But yet it is true; the poorest believer in the world is the heir of all the world.

You will then say, "How can that be?" I would put the question to you, "How was Abraham the heir of the world?"

You will say that you have little of the world. No more had Abraham when the promise was made to him. Abra-

Faith Puts Dignity Upon the Soul

ham had nothing in the land of Canaan but a burying place. He took possession, as it were, of the world by Canaan, and yet he had nothing of Canaan but a mere burying place all his lifetime—yet he was heir of the world. In this way a believer is an heir of all the world; in this way, certainly, he has right to all the good things in the world so far as may be useful to him and good for him.

You who are the poorest, had you more of the world than you have, it may be you would have less grace, if God should put it to your choice. If you knew all, you would not have more than you have, for God takes care to provide that which is best for you, and all things are to turn to your good. If you lack something of this world that others have, yet your want is turned to some spiritual advantage. This I dare affirm, that there is no believer who lacks anything of the world but it is made up in some other way.

But it is not without probability that this Scripture may be made good that believers shall inherit the world, that there is a time coming for believers to inherit the earth, though for the present wicked men for the most part have it now. Why? Because the world is defiled with sin; there is such corruption in the world. But now God is content that even those He hates, and reprobates many of them, should inherit the great things of the world because it is so defiled. But there is a time coming that there shall be a restitution of all things, and the corruptions of the world shall be taken away, and sin taken out of the world, when all shall be purged, and the world made fit for the saints of God, and they shall come to inherit the world. They are the heirs of all the world now, and shall possess the world when God's time shall come.

And the saints are not only heirs, but heirs together with Jesus Christ, co-heirs; and that is a greater dignity that is put upon the saints, and all by faith. It's a great dignity for a man not only to have such an inheritance given to him, but to be joined fellow-purchaser with Him so that it cannot be taken away from him. Truly it is as much to be made a co-heir with Jesus Christ. We have the right to all things by faith, the right of purchase, the right of donation, and the right of inheritance. And this inheritance of being joined to Jesus Christ means that if Christ is a rightful heir of all the world, then believers are rightful heirs. The saints have so much right to all the good things of the world besides heaven that if Jesus Christ is a right heir, then they also are rightful heirs. As a co-heir with the Lord Jesus Christ you have an interest, an interest by your inheritance; and your inheritance is strengthened by the inheritance of Jesus Christ, as He is the heir of all things.

These dignities besides many others, such as being made free of the new Jerusalem which is above, of which such glorious things are spoken in the Scriptures, so many as believed they were added to the church. Oh, precious is that grace that puts such dignities and honors upon the saints as this does, "to those that have obtained like precious faith." And yet there is still more besides all this.

9
Four Additional Reasons Why Faith Is Precious

Faith is that grace that is the cleansing and purging grace, the sanctifying grace. The heart is purified by faith. "And you are sanctified by faith" (Acts 15:9). All the resolutions that men have against their sin will not cleanse their hearts from their sin, does not sanctify them, but faith does. The exercise of faith in one quarter of an hour does more to purge out sin in the soul than all our mourning, sorrowing, and performing duties. Anything in the world done for a long time cannot purge out the filth of sin so much as the exercise will do.

It is faith that renews the image of God in the soul. It's by faith that we live, that we have any life. The Apostle John says, "These things are written that ye might believe that Jesus is the Christ, the Son of God; and that believing, ye might have life through His name" (John 20:31). Yes, he who has the Son has life, but he has it by believing. You know that Scripture in Habakkuk is many times expressed to the Romans and to the Hebrews: The just shall live by faith. Some read it thus, with some difference in points of the word: "The just by faith shall live," or "the just shall live by faith." And the very pointing of the words will make a great deal of difference in the reading of it: "The just by faith shall live" (make a stop there), and "the just (make a stop there) shall live by faith. "The just by faith" (make a stop there), and then it notes that men made just only by faith, and by being made just through faith, now they come to live. They never lived before; they were dead before. Or else thus, the just, one who is just, shall live by his faith; he shall live. So it does not denote being made just by his faith, but he comes to live the very life of God now that he has faith, the life that he has now. I live (said Paul) by the faith of the Son of God; it is by the faith of the Son of God that we come to live, and that life is no other but the very beginning of everlasting life. You have it many times in Scripture, as in John 6:47: "Verily, verily, he that believeth on Me hath everlasting life."

Mark the words we have in many other Scriptures. You think that he who believes in Christ shall have everlasting life; no, not only so, but he who believes in Christ has everlasting life, he has it now. He lives the life of heaven now. He has eternal life beginning now in the soul. It is faith that brings for the present everlasting life. You who before your faith were as dead carrion in the eyes of God, a dead dog, when faith comes into the soul you now stand up and live an eternal life. You have the same life now that the saints have in heaven (the beginning of it). The Kingdom of God has come down into you; heaven has come down into your soul; therefore it is, as in the place before named, that we are made partakers of the precious promises, and by them partakers of the divine nature. We come to have the promises by faith, and by them to have the divine nature into the soul. And this is the preciousness of faith: It cleanses the heart from filth and sanctifies it. It brings new life, everlasting life, the divine nature, it sets up the image of God in the soul, and it puts a principle of eternal life in the hearts of sinners. This is that which faith does.

Yea, faith not only brings all other graces, but all other graces are but the train of faith, and the attendants of faith (as I may so say). But further, it's a grace that puts a quickness upon all graces. When other

Four Additional Reasons Why Faith Is Precious 39

graces begin to abate of their virtue and liveliness, it is faith that puts a quickness into them all. It revives not only a dead soul, but graces that seem to lie dead for the present. Therefore a learned man, Gulielmus Parrisienst, compares it to a crystal, that when all other pearls have lost their vigour and excellence, by the mere touch it recovers the virtue of all precious stones. So faith, when other graces have lost their quickness and activeness, then by faith they are all set to work again, and put into a liveliness and activeness again.

Many Christians have graces, yet many times their graces lie dead in their hearts, and for want of the exercise of faith they lie dead. Those Christians who can exercise faith most are the most lively Christians; they always have their graces fresh, lively, vigorous, and in full virtue of them by the exercise of faith. You may find this by experience, if when you find yourselves dead and dull, and you do not find the virtue of humility and patience, the way is to strengthen your faith and quicken it, and it will stir up all other graces. And that is another excellence. It is precious faith then that has such a precious work in the soul.

And yet further, faith is precious in that as it quickens up all and enlivens all, so it is faith that puts a dignity upon all the works of the saints. Faith makes any work that the children of God do to be noble, and makes all to be acceptable unto God. You know what is said of the faith of Abel in Hebrews 11. You may read there the large commendation of faith: "And by faith Abel did offer a sacrifice more acceptable than that of Cain." What was it that made the sacrifice of Abel more acceptable than Cain's? It was faith. So a man who is not a believer may perhaps do a thing that, for the matter of it, may be as good as a believer does; but this is not acceptable before you are a believer. All that you do is rejected by God; it is rejected in order to eternal life; the Lord does not accept what is done so as to accept it of you for life. He cannot be well pleased with what is done. It's true, there may be something done that may take away some hindrance of the work of faith, but to say that God is well pleased with you cannot be true until you are a believer.

However, do not say, "What, shall we do nothing then, being unbelievers?" For it may be that what is done may be less sin, and materially good, and so it is your duty to do it. You must do whatsoever God requires of you; it's materially good. But take all together, and you cannot be said to please God without faith, for Scripture says, "Without faith it is impossible to please God."

Not only do you not please God, it's impossible to do so. You think that if you have good meanings and good desires, and you are sorry for what you have done, and you come to church and hear the Word, and are just in your dealings with men (and the like), that this will suffice; but this does not please God without faith. It's not possible for you to please God. Do not tell me what you do, but rather tell me the principle by which you do these things. You may live better than you have done. There may be many things in your actions that you have mended; but yet if your state and condition are not changed by being brought into Jesus Christ, that which you do is not accepted. But faith puts an acceptance upon what we do.

Luther had such an expression concerning faith (he who had so much himself, and therefore admired it so much the more): "The actions of the poorest milkmaid, the poorest servant, are more glorious than all that Alexander or Julius Caesar, or those famous conquerors who conquered almost all the world. The actions of the poorest servant in but milking a cow or sweeping a house are more honorable in the eyes of God than those were, if these servants are believers, and do what they do out of faith. It is more honorable because it is out of faith."

For faith not only sets the soul to work to close with God, but sets it on work to perform all things and your duties are accepted by God, and they are a sweet savour in the nostrils of God. That broken prayer of yours, though you are not able in words to express yourself but by breathing and panting out your heart to God, coming from faith, is more accepted than all the glorious works that all the hypocrites in the world do or possibly can do. It is faith that brings acceptance not only to our persons, but to our actions. It ingratiates a person and his duties at the throne of God; and that's a precious grace. Is not that worth a world that shall make our poor, mean, low, nothing-services that we tender up to God to be accepted by Him? This is only by the grace of faith.

10

Faith Enables the Soul to Do Glorious Things

Faith is that which enables the soul to do most glorious things. It not only puts acceptance upon our meanest things, but is that which gives power and strength to the soul to do great things. The meanest believer is able to do great things by faith. You know what great things were done by faith in Hebrews 11. Read that chapter when you go home, for it is suitable to be read after such a sermon as this. It is a little chronicle of faith's worthies and their acts; you may see what glorious actions were done by faith.

But it may be when you read that Scripture, some of you may be discouraged in some things, and think surely we shall never be able to do such things. I desire you to take special notice of one verse there, verses 33–34: "Who through faith subdued kingdoms, wrought righteousness, obtained promises, stopped the mouths of lions; quenched the violence of fire, escaped the edge of the sword, out of weakness were made strong, waxed valiant in fight, turned to flight the armies of the aliens."

Now you will say, "These are great things, but what do these concern us?" Here is a glorious work of faith: "Who through faith subdued kingdoms, stopped the mouths of lions," but mark verse 33, between "subduing kingdoms," and "stopped the mouths of lions," you have here, "wrought righteousness and obtained the promises."

It may be you cannot subdue kingdoms, nor stop the mouths of lions, but you can work righteousness and obtain the promises by your faith. And these two are put in the middle as being of the same nature, as great an excellence as subduing kingdoms and stopping the mouths of lions; and yet who knows what the faith of poor people may do. Though you cannot go into the field to fight against the enemies of the nation, yet by faith you may subdue them and make them your footstool, and stop the mouths of lions that come roaring and raging to swallow up the servants of God.

But particularly what faith can do, such a man is commended for the excellent abilities. "Why, what can he do more than others?" You speak of faith that it is so precious, "Why, what can it do?" It can do this:

1. Prevail as a prince with God in prayer. It's the prayer of faith that can prevail; if any prayer prevails with God, it is through faith. It can overcome God and prevail as a prince with him, to have from God what it would have. "O woman, great is thy faith; be it unto thee as thou wilt," said Christ to the poor woman. It is as if Christ should say, "Nay, woman, if so be that you have faith, and work by faith, there is no gainsaying of you; you may prevail to have anything that you will. Great is your faith, be it unto you as you will."

If any people are set upon their will, oh, they are very willful, why, here's the best way for any man or woman to have their will. It is said therefore of Luther that he could do whatsoever he would do because he was a man so full of faith.

2. Faith is the grace that has the power to resist temptations. In Ephesians 6:16, it's the shield of faith that has the power to quench the fiery darts of the devil. It's a very

strange expression, "the devil's darts." He shoots fiery darts; and faith is not only a shield to fence them off, but to quench the fiery darts.

You may ask, "Why, what power has a shield to quench fire?" Faith has not only strength to beat off darts, but to quench fiery darts. Just as now our national enemies have the art to shoot red hot fire-iron bullets into a town. Just such kind of darts or bolts the devil shoots upon the souls of the saints; and therefore if they do not have a shield that would quench them, they are likely to be overcome. So let the darts of the devil come never so hot, yet faith is the shield that will quench them.

Many of you complain when you are overcome, "Oh, the devil overcame me; the temptations of the devil are strong." Why, how came they to be strong? Because you do not have the right shield to quench them; perhaps you have the shield of resolution, that you will do thus and thus better than ever you have done. Yes, but when it comes to the fiery darts of the devil, they prevail for you have only the shield of your resolutions; you do not have the shield of faith. It is faith that is able to resist temptations, and it is faith that dispels fears. Tertullian has such an expression, "Faith does not fear hunger." And it is faith that overcomes all kinds of fear. This might be shown more largely, but I shall hasten on to the following particulars

3. It is faith that rises above all discouragements; that's the grace that does it, and carries the soul through all kinds of difficulties. There are many things that come the way of the soul to discourage it. It may be that sense says, "It cannot be"; reason says, "How can it possibly be?" and the world says, "It shall not be." But faith comes and says, "It shall be." After reason has concluded against it, and

sense has concluded against it, and all the world has concluded against a thing, faith says "Ah, but for all this it shall be done." It keeps the head above water in the midst of waves and tempests, though the body be under.

The saints of God in former times had discouragements enough had they not been kept up by faith, which we shall show more clearly hereafter. Take both of these in the example of Abraham. What discouragement might Abraham have had in offering up his son, especially that great discouragement, "What shall become of the promise of God?" Well, said Abraham to his servants, "I and the lad will go yonder; you stay here, and I and the lad will go and come again."

Isaac was to be sacrificed and burnt to ashes, and yet Abraham said, "I and the lad will come again." It's as if Abraham should say to Isaac, "I must have you to burn to ashes, but yet I must come again with the lad; and in this child all the nations of the world must be blessed. God has promised, and though he be burnt to ashes, yet he must come again."

Faith will bring a live Isaac out of the ashes; and it is a sign that people are not acquainted with this heroic grace of faith who are so presently discouraged with every little thing. If they meet with a work that is but a little difficult they give over.

Faith will break through difficulties, as in Hebrews 11, about verse 34 and afterwards. You may see what difficulties thousands did break through by their faith. Let the means be never so small that God would have us use, though the means come never so much under the thing we use the means for, yet faith will carry it through. Indeed, it is so much the more glorious by how much weaker the means are, and therefore that's observable in Hebrews chapter 11. You shall find in Joshua's faith, that by faith he did pull down the walls of Jericho. Now sometimes I have wondered with myself why it is that Joshua had faith at one time to cause the sun to stand still in the firmament; but when the Holy Ghost commends his faith He does not say that the sun stood still in the firmament, but by faith the walls of Jericho fell down. I cannot think of any other reason but this, because that was an extraordinary work. Yet Joshua had to deal with God in it in an extraordinary manner, and it was a sudden work of God in the raising of his heart to such faith. But that of Jericho was a thing that had more discouragements as no work could have the like, as could conceive that here is a strong city that had strong walls, and these must fall to the ground. How? He must have a company of priests to tooting and blowing round about the walls; and this must be the means to bring down the walls of the city.

Certainly those in Jericho could not but laugh at them because it was a thing so contrary to sense, and such a poor weak means; but the faith of Joshua is commended so much the more, as if God should say, "Well, my servant Joshua, when I set him about such a work that was so difficult, and all means he had was but a few rams horns to do it, and yet he goes on by faith and believes it, and at length go down the walls of Jericho." So when God sets us about great works, if means fail, or if they seem to come too short, yet faith will carry through all; and this is the honor of it. And if by faith we can be carried through a work, when the means are weak, poor and mean, oh, this is that which God accounts to be honorable. It is the glory of faith to do this.

4. And what can faith do?" you ask. It will rejoice in tribulations, and it knows how to make up all our wants in

God Himself. Let afflictions be never so great, faith knows how to rejoice; faith can see day through a little crevice. In Romans 5, we rejoice in tribulations; other men may be patient in tribulations, but faith makes us to rejoice, and to glory in tribulations. They are a hundred degrees further than patience; it is not enough for a believer to be patient in tribulations, but to rejoice and glory in tribulations, to be exceeding glad.

5. Do you ask, "What can faith do?" It can overcome the world. This is our victory, even our faith, whereby we overcome the world, says the apostle. It lifts the believer above all things in the world, above the favor, frowns, and fears of the world. It overcomes the world, not only because it keeps the world from doing it mischief, but it can make use of the world for its own good. We are more than conquerors through Christ.

6. Would you know what faith can do? It can look upon the face of the holy and just God with joy, and upon the face of death, and of judgment with joy. Let God appear in His infinite holiness and justice before the soul, yet by faith the soul can be enabled to look upon the face of the holy and righteous God with joy. Oh, how precious is this grace of faith! And as we go along we may see that certainly the faith of the greatest part of the world is not true faith; the ordinary common faith is not this true faith. We may have ordinary stones in the street, but this jewel is a rare thing. There are divers things yet that I intended for the opening a little more of the preciousness of this grace.

11

Faith Glorifies God Most

I shall briefly add some few particulars more in faith's commendation, and then come to some application, for indeed the opening of the point has had application in it.

Faith is the special grace that glorifies God; no grace glorifies God so much as faith does. We glorify God by our humility and by our patience. By the exercise of every grace God has honor, but no grace so much honors as faith. Therefore it is said of Abraham in Romans 4 that he believed and glorified God; he glorified God in believing. Hence it is that Christ tells us that this is the work that God would have us to do, even our faith. To believe is the greatest work of all, that which brings glory unto God more than anything else. And the truth is, nothing glorifies God but believing; and other graces, as they have the virtue and excellence of faith in them, so they glorify God's name.

Faith gives glory to God in a peculiar way. It gives Him the glory of many of His attributes together. It gives Him the glory of His truth and faithfulness. God stands much upon the glory of those. It gives Him the glory of His power by resting upon Him, and the glory of His mercy, these three attributes especially. It's a great honor that's put upon God, and the soul-worship that the creature is able to worship God with, for a soul to cast itself and to venture itself for all its present good and eternal good upon a mere word of God, though it sees nothing else for it. Yea, though it sees many things going against it, yet if it has but once a word it can venture its eternal estate upon that word; this is a mighty honor that is given to God. A man would account himself much honored if a man should venture his life and his estate upon a man's mere word, upon a man's faithfulness, that if so be that he should fail him, it would be as much as his life were worth. <u>Why, God accounts Himself exceedingly honored in this, when you can rest your soul upon His mere faithfulness, that in the midst of temptations and of all trials and oppositions, yet you can venture your soul upon Him, and can say, "Though He kills me, yet will I trust Him."</u>

Many poor Christians are afraid to believe; they are not afraid to go to prayer and hear the Word, or to walk in the duties of obedience to other commandments, but when they come to believe they are afraid to believe. Why are you afraid to do that which God accounts the greatest glory to His name of all the things that you can do? God is not so well pleased in any action that you can do as in the action of casting your soul upon Him, and venturing your eternal estate upon His free promise.

And it's a special honoring of God in this because, by the grace of faith, God attains that which His special design is for the magnifying of His own name. And what is the great design that God has in the world but the magnifying of the riches of His free grace? That is what God aims at above all. It's true, if God will have a world, He must put forth His almighty power to make this world; and if He will have a world He must order and guide things in the world to keep them from confusion. In this He magnifies His wisdom; and He must preserve His creature if He means to have a world continue any time; and here He magnifies His goodness.

Yes, but there is a further design that God has in mak-

Faith Glorifies God Most

ing the world; it is that He might have some of His creatures to all eternity magnifying of the riches of His free grace. That's the great design, and all the other things God did here in this world are in some way or another in order to accomplish this.

But the top of all that which God aimed at in making the world is that He might have some creatures that might magnify the riches of His free grace to all eternity. Now what grace in the heart of man serves so immediately for the magnifying of God's free grace as the grace of faith? And how does God attain to the glory of this design of His but by faith? That's the grace that lifts up the glory of God's free grace in His Son; and therefore it is precious, because of all graces it is that which glorifies God. And if Christians did but understand this, were they convinced of this, they would be as much afraid of unbelief as well as fear the sin of theft, or of swearing, or blaspheming, or murder, or adultery.

If there should be a temptation to adultery, or uncleanness, or blasphemy, your hearts would tremble at it. Why? Because you think these are great dishonors to God. Now when there comes a temptation to unbelief, your hearts should shake as much at that; for if faith is the great grace that glorifies God, then unbelief is the great sin that dishonors God in the world.

12

Faith Puts the Believer Into a State of Happiness He Can Never Lose

Faith is a precious grace because it puts the believer into a state of happiness that he can never lose. Now that is precious, and all the graces that Adam had did not put him into such a condition. Adam had the image of God; he was made according to God's image in holiness and righteousness. But all the holiness that Adam had in innocence did not put him into an immutable condition, into an eternal estate, but so as he might lose it; yet faith puts the soul into a state of happiness that it can never lose. Hence it is said that we are kept by the power of God (but it's by faith) to salvation. The power of God does not keep us unto salvation, but by faith the power of God keeps us as in a garrison to salvation. It is faith that makes all other graces so that they cannot be lost, because it catches hold upon such a principle, such a fountain of spiritual life. Here's the ground of it, why the state of a Christian is a state of happiness that cannot be lost, whereas the graces of Adam were.

The reason is this: Adam had grace given to him by God, and the principle of his life was put into him. He had the principle of his spiritual life in him; as a watch has the springs put into it to move, so Adam's graces were put into him as the principle of his life. Now a Christian has grace put into him as Adam, but the principle of his life it is still in another, in Jesus Christ his Head whom he is united to by faith. And faith is the grace whereby the soul goes out of itself to fetch a principle of life, and lives upon a principle of life out of itself, but lives in its head Christ, and so it is not out of itself, that is, out of the same mystical body, but out of itself, out of its own soul.

Faith not only fetches life from Christ at first, but it is the grace that continually fetches life from Jesus Christ the Head. Hence it is that by faith the state of a Christian comes to be better than the state of Adam was in innocence, before he even sinned against God. This is a precious grace, whereby we come not only to be united to the Fountain and Root of life, but whereby we come to fetch a continual supply of life. Therefore certainly a Christian cannot perish because now he lives by a principle of life that is without himself, in Christ, and he has this grace put into him to fetch life continually from Him.

13

Faith Is the Only Condition of the Second Covenant

Faith is precious in this, that it is the only condition of the second covenant. The last thing of all that shows the preciousness of this grace of faith is this: It is the only condition of the second covenant. So God loved the world that He sent forth His only begotten Son, that whosoever believed should not perish, but have everlasting life. The condition of the first covenant was, do this and live; the condition of the second covenant is this, believe and live. Faith is the only condition of the second covenant; therefore it is that which interests the soul in all the rich treasures that there are in the second covenant.

All the good of a Christian consists in the benefit of the second covenant; whatever riches a Christian has, they are the fruit of the second covenant, it comes from that; all the comfort of a saint is in the covenant of grace that God has made with him. And it is faith only that is the condition of the second covenant that God has made with the soul in Jesus Christ. He requires nothing as the condition of it. All the works of preparation that are there before are not at all the condition of the second covenant; neither are the works of sanctification a condition of it. The works of preparation are only such things as without which we cannot come to have faith. Thus, we cannot have faith unless we come to know what Christ is, and we must know that Christ is a Saviour, and what He saves us from. We must be sensible of them, and not only know them, but be affected by them. These are the things that necessarily go before faith, but not as any conditions.

Works of preparation are not the condition of the second covenant. Works of sanctification are the condition of the justified person, but not the condition of justification; they are not the condition of the covenant that God has made with us in Christ. They are rather the fruits of the covenant than the condition of it. All the works of sanctification flow from the covenant, and faith, that is, grace, is the condition of it. And God uses this grace to be the condition of the second covenant, and hereby manifests more the glory of His free grace than before because the creature may not boast, because the covenant may be free. Therefore it is that God has chosen faith to be the condition of the covenant, because it may be free.

If so be that God had chosen other graces, it would not have been so free as by choosing faith, for other graces are graces that are indeed the renewal of that which Adam had in innocence at first, the image of God that Adam had there. But faith goes out of itself to another; that's the proper grace of faith, and therefore this shows the freeness of the covenant of grace more than if other graces had been the condition of the covenant. Faith is but the hand to receive it. It is not the condition of the covenant, as works were before in Adam; neither is it now the condition as a work. It is one of the meanest works in itself, taken in its own nature. It's that which enables man as much as anything that is; it is a grace whereby a man goes out of himself for all his good, and receives it of another. The excellence consists in this, in that it is an instrument to fetch so much good to the soul; there lies the excellence of it.

Faith Is the Only Condition of the Second Covenant

So faith is a condition, but not a condition merely as it is a work in itself, but as an instrument that God has appointed to fetch in from Jesus Christ. Thus it comes to be a condition of the covenant, and this is most suitable to a covenant of free grace, the most suitable condition that possibly could be. Hence it is that God would have this to be the condition of the covenant, because it is sure it could not have been so sure if other graces had been the condition of it, because other graces could not assure the heart of that perfect righteousness to stand before an infinite, just, and holy God, so as this can do. If other graces are weak and have imperfections in them, the soul is presently at a standstill, and does not know what to do. How can they be fit to be tendered up to an infinitely holy God? But now faith, though it is never so weak and imperfect, the soul needs not be at standstill because of this, because it is a hand to fetch in that which is perfect. Now a weak hand may receive a rich jewel as well as a strong hand, but a weak hand cannot work so well as a strong hand; yet a weak hand can take a precious thing as well as a strong hand. Now, I say, the covenant is more sure because faith is the condition of it, for though it is never so weak, yet this is the proper work to fetch and receive in a perfect righteousness.

Now the soul is not liable to so many temptations if it understands things aright upon the knowledge of faith being the condition of the covenant, as when it apprehends other graces to be the condition of the covenant. For example, many who are weak, and do not understand aright the covenant of grace, think indeed that God will have mercy upon them, that is, if they were so delivered from their corruptions, and have so much power against their sins. Or if they were able to perform duties in such and such a manner, then they think God would have mercy upon them. And it is very natural to a man to think that God will have mercy on him upon no other terms than his obedience, his duties, and upon his corruptions that he overcomes. I say, this is very natural. Why? Because it was once the condition of the covenant. God dealt with Adam in a natural way suitable to a rational creature, the first covenant, and the condition of it was that which was suitable to the nature of a rational creature, and so God dealt with him in a natural way.

Now men who are yet in their natural state have some apprehension of God, and would fain have peace with God, and pardon of their sins, are very prone to conceive that they are to deal with God in a natural way. That is, they think, "If I overcome my sins, God will have mercy upon me."

I say, this is to look upon God as if He would deal with me in a natural way, and by this you come to err. But when we come to understand the covenant aright, we understand that God does not show mercy to the soul upon this condition of overcoming corruptions and performing duties—though it's true, wherever there is faith, there will be this. And the soul that comes to understand that God does not deal with the soul upon this condition, but on the condition of going out of itself and believing in a mediator, and to fetch righteousness from another, this helps the soul against many temptations. And one who comes to understand the way of the covenant aright is mightily delivered from any temptations that other Christians are pestered with. Thus the excellence of faith is that it is the only condition of the second covenant.

14

Some Uses of the Doctrine

USE OF INFORMATION. Now to wind up all in a little further application of all, besides that which we have already said, if this is the faith that is spoken of, then certainly faith is very rare, and we might make it to be one particular for the opening of the preciousness of faith. It may appear to be precious on account of it being so rare, as precious stones you know are accounted precious for their rarity. And from what has been said we may very well conclude that faith is precious, as in 1 Samuel 1 at the beginning, where it is said that the Word of God was precious in those days.

Is it not precious in these days? Oh, yes, it's a precious jewel; but in those days the Word was precious, that is, it was very rare; there was very little of the Word of God in those days, and therefore it was precious. So we may well say that faith is a precious grace because there is very little of it; yea, "and when the Son of man shall come, shall He find faith upon the earth?" Little faith will be found upon the earth when Jesus Christ shall come. We all profess ourselves to believe in Jesus Christ, but when Christ, that great Jeweler (if I may so say) shall come to try our precious stone, whether it is right or not, most will prove to be false. And all these particulars that I have opened in the preciousness of faith will be as too many particulars to try our faith.

USE OF COMFORT. The consideration of this point is a matter of exceeding comfort to all the people of God, to all believers upon whom the Lord has bestowed this precious faith. Perhaps the Lord has not bestowed upon you gold or silver, nor given you jewels to hang about your necks to adorn you as others have. Ah, but He has given you this jewel of faith, and indeed this is instead of all. All riches are comprehended in this jewel of faith, and many a poor man or woman to whom God gives but little of outward things, yet in giving faith the Lord makes such a one to be rich. Hence in James 2:5: "Hearken, my beloved brethren," as a thing that should comfort the hearts of poor people, as a thing of wonder and of great comfort, "Hearken, my beloved brethren." So I say to you who are poor in the world, and who have little of the world's riches, hearken to this consolation: "Hath not God chosen you that are poor to be rich in faith?"

Suppose God had given you all the riches of the world and denied you this pearl. You would be a miserable creature without it, but certainly this makes you happy; it is better than all, and by this you may have a supply of all.

Consider these particulars in this use of comfort: This precious jewel of faith is given instead of all riches; it is better than all the riches in the world; it is that which gives you right to all the riches in the world; and it is that whereby you may have a supply of all things according to your necessity. And further, you need not fear any evil, for you have that within your own soul that may help against any kind of evil that possibly can befall you here in this life; and therefore your heart may be comforted. God expects that His saints on whom He bestowed this precious jewel, though they find little else that they have from God, He expects that they should be satisfied in this, and account it a good portion, and a goodly inheritance in that they have such a jewel as this is.

USE OF ENCOURAGEMENT. Further, it may be a mighty encouragement to all those who are seeking after this grace of faith, when they hear what a precious jewel this grace is. Is there anyone whose heart the Lord has begun to strike, that now he is seeking after to get faith? They see the breach that sin has made between God and their souls, and they hear that God has made a gracious covenant of life and salvation to believers, and they think with themselves, "Oh, that I had faith. Oh, that I was but sure that I had faith."

Now you are seeking after it, and would give a thousand worlds (if you had them at your disposal), so that you were sure that you had this grace of faith. It may be you have been seeking long and you do not have the ability yet to believe. Do not be discouraged in seeking it. Though God makes you wait for it a long time in seeking it, it is worth seeking. If you can have it at last you are a made man forever. You hear how precious it is; therefore do not grudge your pains and your labor that you are put upon in seeking after this grace of faith.

Consider what a great deal of labor men take in seeking after pearls; they go to the uttermost parts of the earth and into places where they endanger their lives by the extremity of the heat, and compass the world up and down to enrich themselves with pearls and precious stones. Certainly then you who are seeking for this pearl are as the merchant we read of in Matthew 13:45. He was seeking for goodly pearls and at length he found a pearl of great price, and went and sold all that he had and bought it.

It's true, Jesus Christ is the pearl, and faith is the next, because by faith we come to have our interest in Jesus Christ. Now, if you are willing to part with all that you might have this pearl, and so the other, though you are a long time under the spirit of bondage, and endure much trouble of conscience for many years together, yet if God is all this while working this grace in your soul, you need to be quiet and not murmur. You should not cry out, "Oh, the trouble of conscience that I have. Oh, the long time that I have sat in darkness, and I pray, and nothing comes." If God is working this grace in your soul, though it costs you dearly it will pay the charge. Faith will make amends for all. Therefore when you read or hear anything of this precious grace of faith (any of you upon whom God is now working), God has you under His hand in working upon your hearts; be willing to go on, and though it is many years together before you get it, yet when it does come, it will quit all the cost and pay all the charges, for it's that which will enrich your soul with spiritual riches to all eternity.

USE OF EXHORTATION. Further, upon hearing of the preciousness of this grace, let us all be so in love with it as to be restless till we come to know whether we have it or not.

As for evidences and signs, I do not intend to give any now, because the opening of it included the signs and evidences of it. What are the signs of a precious stone but the very glory and lustre of it? So the very glory and lustre of faith that I have opened are evidences and signs enough. Now let us be restless till we come to find these working, for, the truth is, without this grace of faith all the truths of God vanish and come to nothing. You will certainly depart from your profession if you meet with affliction and troubles and difficulties if you do not have faith in these times in which God has cast you. You are unfit to live in these times if you do not have this precious grace of faith. Therefore be restless in your spirits till you have it.

15

Directions How to Get Faith

You will say, "We shall be restless in our spirits till we get faith? Then how can we get it?"

Here are some rules for obtaining faith:

RULE 1. Faith is the gift of God, yes, but though it is, you know the Scripture says that faith comes by hearing the Word of God. When God gives this precious faith, He usually gives it by hearing; that's the way. Now I know that God is not limited to any one way, but that's God's ordinary way. Do not expect that God will give it to you at your seeking. Where does God say that He will? But God says that faith comes by hearing the Word of God.

Now how precious should God's Word be to you? Take heed of neglecting the Word of God, especially the Word of God that shall lay open the doctrine of the gospel to you, that shall show Jesus Christ unto you. Take heed of neglecting it any one time that God gives you opportunity to enjoy it. Perhaps you are loath to rise in the morning, or neglect some other opportunity. How do you know but that might be the morning that God might intend to give unto you this precious stone?

Many have come, sometimes accidentally, to hear the Word, and the Lord has wrought this excellent grace of faith in them, that they would not for ten thousand worlds have been without. Do not neglect hearing, but wait at wisdom's gates; and though God does not work in one sermon, He may work in another. Therefore let it be your care to attend upon the Word, and to attend for this very end, that God might work faith. "Lord, you have said that faith comes by hearing, and this is a most precious grace. Oh, that my soul might have it when I come to hear Thy Word; for it's the very end that I might have faith wrought by hearing. <u>I come not to hear merely, and to know what such a man can say about such a point, but I come to that very end that God might work faith in my soul.</u>"

Oh, how just might it be with God that those people should perish eternally without faith who will not attend upon the means of obtaining faith. If you will sit at home sluggish, and be busied about base and vile things when others of God's servants are hearing the Word; oh, when you shall come upon your death beds, and then come to cry to God for the pardon of your sins and for faith, oh how just would it be with God to deny it to you (Proverbs 1).

RULE 2. When you do come to hear the Word, you must hear every truth as that which infinitely concerns your souls and your eternal estates. You must come with such a disposition, for indeed that's the reason why people do not have faith, and why they do not believe, because when they come to hear they do not come to hear things as merely concerning themselves. If a man is telling a story, and I think that that which this man tells is a thing that does not so much concern me, then I do not so much mind it as to give credit to it. But if I hear a thing that closely concerns me, then I weigh it, and ponder it, and am easily brought to believe it. Why? Because it is that which so nearly concerns me. So whatever truths you hear, know that they do concern your lives, and therefore weigh and ponder them; and by this God works faith in the soul, for God works it in us (though in a supernatural way), yet He works it in us as rational creatures.

Directions How to Get Faith

RULE 3. When you come to hear the Word, though you cannot find abilities to close with it as you should do, lay up this thought in your minds, and consider if this should prove to be true. "I hear such and such things in the Word about the excellence of Jesus Christ, and of faith, and eternal life, and the glory of heaven, and such things as these are. Indeed I do not have faith enough to see into the reality of these things. Ah, but what if these things should prove to be true? Would I not be a most miserable man to lose all this glory of heaven that I hear of, for the enjoyment of some base sinful lust?"

RULE 4. If you would have God work faith (which is the gift of God), add prayer to your hearing. Before you come prepare by prayer and, when you hear a truth that has any excellence in it, dart up your hearts to God, and with secret ejaculations pray to God that He would cause that truth to sink into your hearts. Then afterwards pray over that truth of God you hear when you are home, and then it may be faith may come. We find it by experience that many people hear truths a hundred times, and yet they do not have faith to close with them. But at length God is pleased to dart them with that power into their hearts so that they cannot but receive them.

RULE 5. Do not give liberty to yourselves to please your senses too much. You know that place in Jude (v. 19) that speaks of men who are sensual, that they do not have the Spirit of God to work faith in the soul. And there's nothing hinders the work of God more than sense. Men who will please senses, and gluttons and unclean persons, and those who give themselves up to live by sense, no marvel that they do not have faith brought into their souls. Sense is a mighty enemy to faith. "We walk by faith, and not by sight (that is, by sense)," said the apostle. Therefore take heed of sensuality; be willing to beat down your body, and not to please your senses too much, and that will be a way for you to get faith in your souls.

RULE 6. You must not only deny sense, but you must deny your reason too. Take heed of attributing too much to your own apprehension. Do not therefore cast off a truth of God because you cannot understand it. Do not reject it because you do not see the reason of it, and cannot understand how it should be. Oh, take heed of that, I beseech you. Luther had such a speech: "Man's corrupt reason is a terrible enemy to faith; faith has no greater enemy than the corrupt reason of man, and this is the ground why many great scholars are left by God." And our Savior said in Matthew 11:25: "I thank Thee, O Father, Lord of heaven and earth, because Thou hast hid these things from the wise and prudent, and hast revealed them unto babes."

The wise of the world stick upon their own reason and their own conceits, and we know that God confounds the wisdom of the world. God has so ordered things in His Word that they should be altogether above reason. And those who stick so much upon their own reason, and their own natural parts, come to be offended with the things of the gospel. They are ready to say as Nicodemus did when Christ told him of the new birth, "How can these things be?" Here's the ground why those who are poor are rich in faith. Why? Because they are poor and weak in their natural parts, and therefore they do not stick so much to their own reason and are more capable subjects for God to work faith upon than others who stick so much to their own parts. Many who have wit and parts are ready to scorn the truths of the gospel that come in plainness and simplicity, as the scholars in Athens scorned Paul's plain preaching of Jesus Christ. But God has so ordered this on purpose that it might be a stumbling block to those, as Christ crucified was to the Jews.

RULE 7. If you would have God to work faith, this precious faith in your hearts, do not sin against that historical faith that God has given you. There's many who, though they do not have this precious faith, yet have another kind of faith. These God has gone on so far in their souls that He has convinced them of the truth of the Scriptures. Though they do not have faith to unite their hearts to Jesus Christ, yet they have so much faith to believe that most things the minister speaks are true. Oh, take heed of sinning against this historical faith, if you would ever come to have justifying faith.

Many a man comes to hear the Word, and believes that those who walk thus and thus shall not inherit eternal life; and many go away, and sin against the very light of their own consciences. And because of this God leaves their souls forever in unbelief, so that they shall never come to have justifying faith to unite their souls to Jesus Christ. Observe this rule whenever God convinces your souls of any one truth in His Word: Go away and charge this truth upon your souls. "O Lord, Thou has convinced me of this truth, and I dare not sin against it."

Now such a soul that dares not do so, such a soul is not far from the Kingdom of Heaven. Though you cannot work this precious faith in your own souls, you need not wilfully go and sin against any light that God puts into your hearts. Those who sin against the light of conscience, it's just with God to deny to them this precious faith that might save their souls.

16

Another Use of the Doctrine

Only one use more shall be considered of the preciousness of faith, namely if faith is so precious, then what a great pity it is that those who have it should not make use of it. God has given precious faith unto many believers, and yet they make little use of it. Solomon said, "It is a grief to see a man who has riches, and not to know how to use them." Likewise, it is a grief to see a believer have faith and know but little how to use it. Therefore, you who are believers, seeing that God has bestowed this precious faith upon you, make use of it upon all occasions. God loves to see the exercise of the grace of faith, and for this reason you should often exercise this grace of faith. I say this because you hear that Christians usually, when they come to any trials, into any great afflictions, or under any temptations, whereas the first thing that they should do should be to exercise their faith; and the main thing that they should do should be to put their faith to work, but you shall observe that the first thing, and the chief thing that they do, is to loosen and to give liberty to themselves to such thoughts as may most weaken their faith.

For instance, suppose a believer comes to a great affliction that God lays upon him. Herein what should he do? He should presently let out his faith and exercise it; the main work of his soul should be to let out in the exercise of his faith. But I appeal to you, when you come to any great affliction, what is it that your hearts are most busied about? If you examine it, it is that which most weakens

Another Use of the Doctrine 67

your faith. You immediately begin to call all into question. "I am afraid I have been but a hypocrite all this while." And presently your sins flies in your faces, and your consciences accuse you, and you are poring upon your corruptions, and beholding how vile you are. It's true, I grant these things are good, to look into your hearts, and to consider your hypocrisy; these things should be done to humble you, but the strength of your souls should be exercised about your faith.

It's the ordinary way of Christians, and yet certainly a deceitful way, it's that which the devil exceedingly troubles Christians with, that when God expects that they should put forth their faith, the main thing that they do is to spend the strength of their spirits about those things that only serve to weaken their faith. Take heed of this, I beseech you, and seeing God has given you this faith, make use of it upon all occasions. And the reason because of this second point, I am but poor and weak. It's true, those who are eminent in faith, when trials and temptations comes, they put forth their faith.

17

The Second Doctrine Opened

DOCTRINE 2. The faith of the weakest believer is equally precious with the faith of the strongest. "To you that have obtained like precious faith."

That's the next point. What do you say that others may do? But what can you do? Your faith is like precious faith with Abraham, Isaac, and Jacob, with any of the apostles, or with the martyrs. I might give you various Scriptures about that, such as "One faith, one Lord, one baptism." And in 1 Peter 5:13 it is said of the church of Babylon that they obtained the like election with us in the city of Babylon (not spiritual Babylon). They had election together with others. As the election is the same with all saints, so their faith is of the same nature. As such, it's equally precious, like precious.

1. It is wrought by the same almighty power, the faith of one and the faith of another. There was as almighty a power put forth in working faith in your soul as was put forth in working faith in Abraham's soul, or Peter's or Paul's soul. Your faith cost (if I may so say) God as much as the faith of any of His servants who ever lived upon the face of the earth, and is equally precious. Your faith is as truly an argument of God's election as the faith of Abraham was, or any of the apostles.

2. Your faith justifies you as much as the faith of Abraham, Isaac, and Jacob, though there may be a difference in sanctification; for a weak faith does not sanctify as much as strong faith, but it justifies as much as a strong

faith. What, has God made me like and equal with them in the point of justification? Had not I need to labor to be as like them as I can in the point of sanctification? That's the main thing upon which my eternal estate depends, the pardon of sin and the saving of my soul; therefore it is like precious faith with them.

3. Your faith as truly interests you in God and unites you to Jesus Christ as the strongest faith in the world; it as truly makes you one with Jesus Christ, and God to be your portion, and the world to be your inheritance, as the strongest faith.

4. Your faith as truly brings you to such privileges to be a child of God and an heir. You are as truly an heir to life and salvation as ever Abraham was, and your faith as truly sanctifies you as the faith of the strongest, though not so much.

5. Your faith as truly interests you in the covenant as the faith of the strongest. You are as truly brought into the covenant as David or Daniel, or any of those eminent ones were. And your faith is of as everlasting a nature as the faith of the strongest, of such a nature as shall never fail as well as the faith of the strongest. I mean by everlasting that it brings you into such a condition as you shall never fall off from Jesus Christ. Oh, you think that those who have strong faith whatever temptations come, they may keep close to Christ and shall never fall off. Believer, be of good comfort; if you have but the least dram of true faith, you are as sure not to be rent from Jesus Christ as ever Abraham or any of the apostles were. It is as impossible for you to be rent from Jesus Christ by the devil as Abraham or Paul, or any of the apostles; and you are sure to come to heaven as any of those.

OBJECTION. Ah, but you will say, "This thing will be a means to make people to be slothful and sluggish. If the least degree of faith will do all these things as truly as the strongest, then what great matter is it whether we have weak faith or strong faith? We may come to heaven if we have but weak faith."

ANSWER. Oh, such reasoning is unworthy of a believer. Have you your faith only for your own ends, because your sin may be pardoned, and you may come to heaven? Is that all the preciousness of your faith? You heard that your faith was precious because it enabled you to give glory to God. In these things you may be equal with others of God's people, but you cannot bring so much glory to God as one who has a strong faith can.

A strong faith will bring a great deal more comfort than weak faith; and though a weak faith may bring to heaven yet with a great difficulty, it will bring you to heaven. As in your ships, would any man reason after that manner? I have seen a poor tattered ship that has had all the sails rent in pieces, and the masts been broken with storms and tempests, yet it has gotten with much ado to the haven, and has not been sunk. Would a man say, It does not matter about my sails, and it does not matter about my masts, so long as I get to the haven." Is there not a great deal of difference between that ship and another with its top-gallants up, and all the sails spreading, and with much safety and ease? Surly this is a great deal better, and so is like Christians going to heaven.

There are many saints who have but little faith, and temptations rend, and tear, and pull them. They are afraid that every wave and billow will swallow them up. Sometimes they are up, and sometimes they are down, and yet

The Second Doctrine Opened

God with His almighty power at length beings them to heaven.

But there are other Christians who come with their full sails to heaven, wind and tide on their side, and they overpower all temptations that come in their way. Is not this a more glorious sight, to see a Christian go with full sails to heaven, and let whatever difficulties or temptations come in the way he can bear them all down?

You shall have other Christians who are continually doubting and fearing, and yet may have that faith that may bring them to heaven, but that dishonors God much and blemishes their holy profession.

But there are others who live above themselves and above the world, and so they glorify God and glorify their profession. You who have weak faith will be ready to stumble upon every thing; as a weak man, he will be ready to stumble at every thing. But a strong man can go on and not stumble. So a weak faith will be ready to stumble at every thing, but a strong faith will not, and therefore let not that reasoning be among you.

18

The Application of the Second Doctrine

USE 1. This may be a great comfort to believers; it may be that you do not have the same precious gifts that other men have; you do not have the like memories. You say, "Such a saint has an excellent memory. Oh, that I had the like." Well, but though you do not have the like precious memory, yet you have the like precious faith that such a saint has. So though you do not have the like natural understanding that other men have, yet you have the like precious faith still.

Set this against the difference that God has made between you and others in other things. God has made a vast difference between you and other people in parts, in estates in the world. Oh, what a difference is between you and them in these things. But now God has made so great a difference between you and others in these things that are not so necessary and excellent, yet in that which is the choice excellence of all things, there God has made no such difference. You have the like precious faith as well as them, and will do the same thing in many particulars as theirs will; and therefore comfort yourselves when you see what differences God has made between you and between others. Sometimes when men and women do but look upon others in whom God has made a great difference between them and us, it affects the heart much. Know, though outward things may seem to make a great difference between man and man, aye, but this is a greater difference. Faith or no faith, that is what makes the great difference between man and man; it is a discriminating grace. Therefore, if God has given you any faith, know that there is no man in the world that is at any great distance from you. Yea, the truth is that there is not a very great difference between you and a saint in heaven, and therefore comfort yourself in that.

USE 2. In the second place, we may see that the faith of most is surely not true faith, because it is not like precious faith with the saints. You may say you have faith, but is it the same faith that Abraham, Isaac, Jacob, and Paul had, the same as the worthies had? Certainly, if it is faith that will carry you to heaven, it is the same faith. But, if it comes to be examined that your faith is but the same faith of Herod's, now what was his faith? Herod heard John, and heard him gladly. Has your faith gone further than his? You come to hear the Word, and perhaps believe and hear it gladly. Ah, but Herod's faith stood with one particular beloved lust. Suppose there is any man who comes to the Word, and hears what is said, believes many things, and rejoices in them, who would not lose a sermon for a great pearl, and reforms in his family, who lives a great better than he did before. Before he was very wicked, perhaps a drunkard, and never prayed in his family. And now after the Word comes to him he leaves off bad company and performs family duties (blessed be God we cannot but say there is a great deal of reformation among many of you). Aye, but mark, yet do you live in any one beloved sin? Is there any one known way of wickedness in you?

You think, "We are all sinners, and I hope God will be merciful unto me in that one thing."

Know this first, that your faith is none other than

Herod's faith was. It is not like Peter's, or Paul's, or Abraham's faith; the weakest degree of faith is the like faith with theirs.

USE 3. Again, you say you have faith, but whose faith is it like? It may be that it's not beyond the faith of the devils. You know that the Scripture says that the devils believe and tremble. You hope you have faith to be saved in Jesus Christ. Why, what does it do?

You can say, "I thank God when I come to hear the Word. I find it strikes to my very conscience, and my heart shakes and trembles."

This is good, but is this all? This is but the same faith with the devils, for the word says that they believe and tremble; and it may even be that you never came that far.

Is your faith like Abraham's and Paul's and Peter's faith? You come and hear terrible truths, truths that should shake your hearts and consciences, and you can go away laughing and scorning. Your faith is not even as excellent as the faith of the devils. Read over Hebrews 11 and see what faith did there, and see whether yours is like precious faith. Perhaps you think you believe in Jesus Christ, but if you come in any place among wicked company who scorn at religion, or that you may suffer much though they had not obtained the promises, yet how they wandered up and down, and suffered torments and mockings (and the like). Now if you have like precious faith with all the saints, then in some measure you may be enabled to do what they did.

USE 4. If the faith of the weakest is the same with that of the strongest, then there is nothing that we read in Scripture that any believer did but every one should labor to get to the height that they did. You will say, "All cannot do alike." But what hinders them? Their faith was as weak as yours, so how did they get up so high to suffer such great things as they did? It was the truth of their faith that carried them through more than flesh and blood could effect. And their faith being true, by using means they got up to those degrees. Now seeing your faith is of the same stamp, why may you not get up to the same degrees? Their hearts were at first as naught as yours, and no better before they had faith. But if their hearts were better after, it was by faith that they bettered them; and they had but the same means, nay, certainly, you who live in the noonday of the gospel light have far greater means than those you read of in Hebrews 13, which is a little "Book of Martyrs."

You are troubled and ready to think you have engaged yourselves too far in the cause of God, because you are afraid of your estates being taken away from you. Yet see by faith that they were carried to wander up and down in sheep skins and goats skins, in leather britches and jackets, being destitute, afflicted, tormented, and yet they continued in their excellence still. Their faith made them so precious that the world was not worthy of them. And they not only lived in faith, but they died in faith, and they obtained a good report.

Now I appeal to your consciences, can you think that any of those that the apostle speaks of there had the like means of the revelation of Jesus Christ that you have? They had not any one thing that is written in the New Testament, for they lived in the time of the Macabees, and indeed the worst times of all, for they neither had prophets nor apostles to be their helps; they had none of the New Testament to be their guide.

Now what a shame is it that any believer, though never so weak, should think that his faith should not do as much as their faith did. Therefore let this consideration prepare you for sufferings if God calls you to it, for you have the same faith, and a clearer day of grace to work in. Thus, whatever they suffered, think with yourselves, "Why may not I suffer, through Jesus Christ strengthening me, as much as they?" Do not be discouraged, for you do not know what faith will do; it was nothing but faith that carried these Christians through the worst of times and the greatest of sufferings.

Yet you may say, "Oh, but their hearts were not as bad as my heart." Well, if they were not, it was only faith that made them better. They did not have like precious means as you have, and therefore God expects that your like precious faith must do and suffer great things if called as they were thereunto.

USE 5. Let all Christians who think they are higher than others in their graces learn to have an honorable esteem of their brethren, though they have less degrees of grace than themselves. Do not condemn them, nor carry yourself aloof from them, but let there be an honorable esteem of Christians, and a loving carriage of one Christian towards another upon this ground: they have like precious faith. It may be you were in the faith sooner than they, yes, but they have gotten the like faith that you have. You have more gifts than they, true, but they have like faith with you. You have a great many in these times of light that if they have attained a little more notional brain-knowledge than some of their brethren in some new point of speculation that others have been acquainted with (though when it comes to be examined it is an old error) they are ready to condemn all other godly people as a company of poor silly novices, as those who are unworthy of being in their company. Well, take heed what you say; it may be you have more conceit than they have.

It may be that such a poor soul has not only like precious faith (if you have any at all), but abundantly more than you have. Certainly, there is many a poor brokenhearted soul that the world little takes notice of who honors God more by believing than a hundred of your talking Christians whose greatest part of religion lies in their tongues. Therefore do not lift yourself up because of your gifts and parts, but look upon others as having the like precious faith that you have. That place in James 2 at the beginning is remarkable: "My brethren, have not the faith of our Lord Jesus Christ, the Lord of glory, with respect of persons." There are some who prefer the word "glory" to "faith" there, and, indeed, the original language is not against it: "My brethren, have not the faith of our Lord Jesus Christ, of glory, with respect to persons." The words "the Lord" there you may see written in other letters, is not in the Greek, but only the translators put that word in to make up the sense. Therefore the words are to be read thus: "My brethren, have not the faith of our Lord Jesus Christ, of glory, in respect of persons." Now this may be referred to faith, as if he should say, "If there is any who has faith, he has glory, for he is a member of Jesus Christ." And again, "Do not have the glorious faith of our Lord Jesus Christ in respect of persons; if there is any degree of faith, it is glorious and precious faith. Do not have it not in respect of persons."

Paul, who was so strong in faith, how did he cry to the Romans? Oh! Paul saw that he had need of the Romans. As we know, little chips will kindle great blocks; and so many Christians who have great strength and great parts, yet your weak Christians many times put life and quickening into their hearts; and therefore the strongest saints should not disdain to converse with the weakest of all, because they are graced and spirited alike for the truth of grace; and therefore they should not disdain to converse with them, and so live in unity and love with one another.

That's the apostle's argument in Ephesians 4. He would have the unity of the Spirit kept in the bond of peace, and makes this argument: "For there is but one Father, and one faith, and one baptism, and therefore keep the unity of the Spirit in the bond of peace." It may be we are not of the same opinion one with another, yet there is a oneness of faith between us; perhaps one man is of this opinion and another of that, but can you see faith? It is said of [Martin] Bucer that if he could see anything of Christ in a man, that alone was the magnet that drew out his love. It is a most miserable and horrible sign of God's displeasure against us that if there is but any difference in opinion one from another, Christians are so estranged that they make no use of one another's graces.

But till we come to learn this, though we are of different judgments and opinions, yet still to make use of one another's graces, questionless things will never be well if men speak of divisions, and say the world will never do well so long as there are so many opinions, and there must be a course taken to bring all men to one way; certainly this is a mistake. This is a dangerous principle, to think that there can be no peace without uniformity of worship. But this is the principle that will cause peace, that is, though there men are of various ways, of various opinions, and of different judgements, yet they have all one faith. And let us make use of one another's graces, and have communion one with another though there are not the like opinions and the like ways. This will cause peace in churches and in commonwealths, whereas the other will never do it; for certainly the judgements of men cannot be forced. But

The Application of the Second Doctrine 79

when there is walking in love and peace one with another, that's the way to bring one another to their judgements, and not by keeping at a distance one from another. A sight of the different ways of people makes some dream that one shall go to heaven in one way and another in another way. No my brethren, there is but one faith, and therefore look what the carriages of God's people were in former times—they are the same now.

You shall observe it, a Christian who lives in one place, and he has occasion perhaps to travel forty or fifty miles, and he meets with a godly, gracious heart that (it may be) he never saw before in his life; but by the time they have been half an hour together, their hearts close together, and they find the very same spirit in them. It is observed in the instruments of music, let one string of a lute be raised up to one height, the other the same, lay a straw upon one and touch the other, and that which has the straw upon it, that sympathizes with it, and the straw will shake and fall off, merely with the consent of the other string that is just of the same kind. So it is with the hearts of God's people, because their graces are all the same and sympathize one with another, and close with another and join sweetly together.

You shall observe it in wicked men: there is the very same spirit of wickedness in all ages. Look how the spirits of wicked men work their hatred and malice. You shall find that they go the very same way in this generation as they did before. Go to one town, and there you shall have one kind of wicked men opposing the saints, and scorning at them; then go to another town and those wicked men there go on in the same road. And so it is from one age to another. Wicked men have the same spirit of wickedness, the same cursed spirit that works in them, and therefore they can join together and company together, because they have the same spirit of Satan that acts in them. Oh! Why should not the saints as well join together, and love and help one another, for they have the same precious grace. Consider what has been delivered, and may the Lord give you understanding in all things.

Finis

The Saints' Walk by Faith on Earth and by Sight in Heaven

"For we walk by faith, not by sight" (2 Corinthians 5:7)

1
The Scope and Meaning of the Words

The apostle, in the latter part of the former chapter and the beginning of this one, shows what it was that carried him and the rest of the suffering saints through the great and manifold afflictions they met with in their way to heaven. This is evident in verse 17 of chapter 6 by that elegant antithesis and double hyperbole beyond English: "For our light affliction, which is but for a moment, worketh [or prepares] for us a far more exceeding and eternal weight of glory." Then in the next verse: "While we look not at the things which are seen, but at the things which are not seen" (verse 18). It was the exercising of their eye of faith upon the things that were not seen; and what those things are that are not seen are shadowed out in the beginning of this 5th chapter: "We know that if our earthly house of this tabernacle were dissolved, we have a building of God, an house not made with hands, eternal in the heavens, and this we groan for, being burdened with sin and misery." Then in verse 6: "We are always confident, knowing that whilst we are at home in the body, we absent from the Lord." We do not enjoy that of God that we do expect, but yet we are confident; for however things seem to work sadly in respect to us outwardly, yet still we have confidence of the great things that are to come. "For we walk by faith, and not by sight." That's the scope.

We Walk: That is, the constant course of our hearts and of our lives is acted and guided by faith, and not by sight. That's the meaning of the words.

Not by Sight: Sight is taken either largely for sense, not only of the eye, but for all other senses both internal and external, one being put for all. We do not walk by sense and especially by the sight of our eyes. Now this sight or sense has a twofold consideration:

First, considered as carnal sense: We do not walk according to what we see with our eyes before us; we do not guide and steer our course according to this.

Second, which is what I think the apostle as truly intends as the other, we do not walk by spiritual sense either, that is, in what we feel in respect of spiritual things. No, we have a principle to guide and act us not only beyond carnal sense, but even beyond spiritual sense; we are guided and acted by faith, for that's the higher principle. And this indeed is a blessed walk of a Christian. He most blessedly walks with God when he comes to be guided and acted by a principle higher than either carnal or spiritual sense.

Again, by "sight" is not only meant sense, but reason. But although this is a higher principle than sense, we do not walk according to the sight of our understandings. Now this, likewise, has a twofold consideration:

First, carnal reason. We do not walk according to the carnal reason of our minds, as if we were acted by nothing else but what we apprehend by our own natural reason.

Second, we do not walk by our spiritual reason only, for we have a principle beyond spiritual knowledge. When I come to that point I shall show how this is meant, not only beyond natural knowledge, but also beyond spiritual knowledge, for faith goes higher than these. Now, that both spiritual sense and spiritual knowledge are meant is clear to me from what the apostle says here: "While we are present in the body,

The Scope and Meaning of the Words

we are absent from the Lord," for we walk by faith and not by sense. Though now we have a confidence and we have some knowledge of God and of what we shall enjoy in Him, but he says we are absent from Him; thus we do not have that sense of it fully as we shall have. Neither do we have the knowledge of it fully. But our faith goes beyond our sense of the presence of God and goes beyond our knowledge of God. We rise higher by our faith than we can by our knowledge, and not only natural knowledge, but also that spiritual and sanctified knowledge that the apostle had, for it did not reach so high as his faith did. Thus you see the scope and meaning of the apostle. In the opening point we shall see it further.

2

The Text Opened

First, we shall treat the negative, what a Christian does not walk according to in the way of his heart or life, not according to sight. Second, we shall treat the positive, by what a saint on earth does walk: He walks by faith. And, third, we shall treat how this walk by faith is beyond sight.

The Negative: A Christian does not walk by sight; he does not walk by sight as other men do. This implies that other men walk by sight, but those that are saints do not. Worldings steer their course and guide their way here in this world according to sight. First, they do this by the sight of their eyes and their other senses; they make that to be their way. Second, they make natural reason to be their guide and go no further. But a Christian is beyond all these, yea, he is beyond his spiritual sense and sanctified reason and knowledge.

First, I will open to you what it is to walk by sight, that is, what men do when they walk by faith. Second, I shall show you that they do so; third, what a great evil there is in walking by sight; and fourth, that the saints do not do as they do.

When I say that the men of the world that are carnal walk first by sense and then by reason, I mean this:

The great good or end that a carnal heart propounds to itself is some good that is the object of sense; for in a walk there is propounding an end whether you would walk to. Now those who are carnal and natural, the end that they propound to themselves is some sensual good.

They judge things according to sense, and their hearts are taken and affected with things according as they are to sense.

Last, though they sometimes have some good motions to that which is beyond sense—sometimes they may have some convictions and sometimes some good affections rising in them; as the morning cloud and early dew—yet the constant way and tenure of their hearts is according to sense. And so they set their lives and actions according to what they see, what they feel.

The end they propound to themselves is the good of sense. The rule by which they judge is sense; that which takes their hearts, it is sense; and the main work of their lives is for some good of sense. And though they have some convictions and some affections sometimes beyond sense, yet the constant bias and stream of their hearts is according to sense. This is a description of a great many men and the course of most people, and I fear that many of your consciences will tell you that this has been your way.

Wicked men are set upon the sight of their eyes. Esau "saw the pottage that it was red," and was taken with the sight of his eyes. He acted by sight, for the priviliges of birthright were beyond sight and he did not order his course according to that, that indeed was an object of his faith. But the pottage was so red that the text says "he saw it," and so he went according to that. And the Holy Spirit in Hebrews 12:16 brands him as a profane man and bids all take heed of being profane as Esau was who sold his birthright for a mess of pottage. Hence he is four or five times branded with "This is Edom," and many such Edomites nowadays prefer earth before heaven, a swine sty before a sanctuary as the gardens, their part in Paris before their part in paradise, as the carnal cardinal. Theotimus said, "Farewell eyes' if I may not drink and do worse, you are no eyes for me." He would rather lose his eyes than sin. Oh, take heed of sensualness.

In the epistle of Jude verse 19, the apostle makes a sensual man and one who does not have the Spirit to be all one, noting that every man who does not have the Spirit of God to act and guide him is sensual and led according to sense. "These are they who separate themselves as sensual, having not the Spirit." I confess that the word in the original includes both these things that I am speaking of, walking according to sense and according to natural reason; and it is the same word that is used for a natural man in Corinthians. "A natural man perceiveth not the things of God." He is a man who is acted by sense and has merely natural apprehensions of things.

Wicked men are carried by sense, both young and old. In Ecclesiastes 11:9 we read: "Rejoice O young men in thy youth and let thy heart cheer thee in the days of thy youth, and walk in the ways of thy heart and in the sight of thy eyes." Now you say, "Here young men are bidden to walk according to their hearts and according to the sight of their eyes." Yes, but it is in a way of irony; it carries with it a severe reprehension: "Do so if you dare."

It's like God said to Balaam: "Rise up and go to Balak" (Numbers 22:20), that is, "Go, if you think it is good; go if you will, but you will go upon your death." Let no man imagine that it ever came in the preacher's heart here to add fuel to the fire of youthful lusts, to entice young people (unruly enough of themselves) to take their full swing of sinful pleasures. But by an ironic concession the wise man bids the young man rejoice; he yields him what he would have by way of mocking and bitter scoff, as Elijah jeered the Baalites and bid them to cry aloud unto the their drowsy or busy god. Likewise, as Micah bade Ahab, "Go up against Ramoth Gilead and prosper," or our Savior bade His disciples: "Sleep on now and take your rest" (Mark 14:41) if you can, or have any mind to it with so many Bils and Halberts about your ears. So the preacher seems to speak, as in former times you use to say to those you would reprimand sharply; "Yes, go on and do what you will and see what will come of it at last." That's the meaning of the text.

Young men, you are set upon the ways of your own hearts, according to sense and the sight of your eyes. You see a great deal of bravery and gallantry in the world and whereby you shall come to live brave and merry lives; your minds are upon that and you will walk according to the sight of your eyes. Like when you see other young men brave, merry, and gallant in the world, oh, you think that's a brave life. Well, go on, but remember God will bring you to judgement for all this. It notes that their hearts are mightily set to do according to what is suitable to their own spirits. The sight of the eyes is what the Apostle John calls covetousness; there's the lusts of the flesh, the pride of life, and the sight of the eyes.

The world is much acted upon by the sight of the eyes; for riches, that's the sight of the eyes, and pleasure here in this place in Ecclesiastes is living according to the sight of one's eyes. And this is the way of carnal hearts. They live according to sense, that is, they see things that are before them suitable to the flesh and that takes their hearts; they see what the world runs after and their hearts are upon them. Then they see the saints, how they suffer hard things. Those who walk most strictly, yet they suffer as hard things as any; and they see that wicked men who live according to the flesh prosper as well as any. These things are before them in sight, and this takes their hearts much; and whatever is said to the contrary they see it and are sensible of the pleasure and delights of the flesh. Now that which is the object of sense is real and certain to them; but as for that of faith, that they look upon as a notion and imagination.

And then the things of sense are present; they enjoy them now. But the things of faith must stay, for they know not when and to have them they cannot tell how. But for those of sense, they see they may have them at present and they find them good unto themselves, and upon this they walk according to sight.

3

The Great Evil of Walking by Sense

Now this is a very great evil, for men to have their hearts taken by what they see with their eyes, and by what their senses tells them to be pleasant and delightful to them. Oh, that I could but make you see the evil of this that an abundance of good might come out of it; for certainly it's this that is the undoing of thousands and thousands of souls. This thing that I am here treating is the undoing almost of all the world; they walk by sight and sense. Oh, how many have been deluded this way, and at length they have come by their woeful experience to see the evil of this! When they have been upon their sick bed and death bed, what has been that which they have cried out of most? "Oh, such things were so pleasant to sense and my thoughts; they were so fine and brave to my eyes and I was carried by that, and now God shows them otherwise to me." Oh, that we could but apprehend things now as one day we shall apprehend them. Truly that man or woman has received great mercy from God who now has the same apprehension of things as one day they shall. There is great evil in this, to go according to the sight of the eyes, for these reasons:

REASON 1. It is beneath a rational creature. What has God set reason in man for but to correct their sense, and especially in matters that concern their chief good. I beseech you to observe it: Reason is a great help to correct sense in many things.

As you know, in natural things reason can correct sense. A country man who is only carried by sense thinks that the sun is no bigger than his cart wheel, for by sense it appears no bigger. But those who understand the principles of astronomy can demonstrate as plainly as two plus two is four that the sun is bigger than the whole earth. Reason will correct sense in natural things, and reason certainly will help much to correct sense in things that concern man's happiness and man's everlasting good, especially when it comes to be sanctified. But reason, at least negatively, will show a man wherein his happiness consists. It will tell us certainly that the happiness of one who has an immortal soul does not have the same happiness that a brute has. To eat and drink, it's not to play. Certainly God has not given a man a rational and immortal soul merely that it should be serviceable to the body only, to be (as the philosopher says of the soul of the swine) as salt to keep the flesh from stinking. Reason will tell a man that there is a higher good that man is capable of than sense, for that's but common with a brute beast. Therefore, it's a great evil to be acted by sense.

REASON 2. Then if it is below a rational creature, oh, how much is it beneath the Holy Spirit of God, that is the Spirit of wisdom and holiness? Now if you are guided by sense:

First, you will have heathens to be witnesses against you that are acted by a higher way, that of reason.

Second, you are then infinitely beneath those who are moved to act by God's Spirit. Are you the man or woman who has the Spirit of God dwelling in you to be your guide continually? If ever you are saved, I say you must be acted and guided by the Holy Spirit of God.

The Great Evil of Walking by Sense

REASON 3. Whoever walks by sight, they are liable to thousands and thousands of temptations continually. Oh, the danger that they are in of temptations, what a snare they walk upon! The senses of men are the wide doors by which the devil comes into their souls. He comes in to the rational soul by the senses first, and if he gets into the senses and prevails there he will get into the reason and prevail there. The eyes, oh, what casements are they to let the devil in by. How many men and women (as the Scriptures said) have eyes full of adultery that cannot cease from sin? When you look upon a woman to lust after her you have committed adultery in your heart, said Christ. Oh, those casements let in wonderful evil to the soul! What was that which let in the first temptation that ever was in the world? It was the sight of the eyes. Eve saw the fruit; she saw it was desirable for knowledge. Thus the first temptation that ever was in the world was let in by the sight of the eyes. Oh, brethren, take heed of the sight of the eyes, for the devil comes in there. You are not willing to leave open your doors and casements in the night where thieves may come in, so you bolt and shut them. You have wooden windows to keep your casements so that they do not come in there. Oh, we need to be careful of our eyes; we need to have something to shut them so that the devil does not come in there. Oh, the wonderful uncleanness and filthiness that comes in by the sight of the eyes! Likewise, at all other senses there comes in a great deal of evil. And so when the devil see that a man or woman is carried by sense, he can easily prevail with temptations. Oh, it's a dangerous thing for people to live by sense!

Then, if you live by sense you are very unlikely ever to come to good, for the way of God in bringing men to eternal life is a way high above reason, as shall be shown, but much more above sense. It is not above only, but contrary to sense; and therefore if you are a man who is given to your appetite, given to follow the light of your eyes, given to sense, it's very unlikely that you should come to anything that's good. Hence it is that those who are led by sense have very light thoughts of the ways of God, and they are the great scorners and enemies of religion. We read in Philippians 3:18: "For many walk" (he speaks of those who walk by sense), but who are they? They are "enemies to the cross of Christ, whose end is destruction, whose God is their belly, and whose glory is their shame, who mind earthly things" (verse 19). These are they who are enemies to the cross of Christ, for sense hinders reason; much more does it hinder grace. In Hosea 4, you read of those who lived according to sense: "Whoredom and wind, and new wine take away their hearts" (verse 11). They are not capable of receiving good while they live according to sense. I will not enlarge myself to treat of a sensual life, but only touch it to show the evil of living according to sense.

It stupefies men extremely; such men as live according to sense have extremely miry and dulled spirits. We read in Ezekiel 47 of those waters of the sanctuary, that they had power to heal. But in verse 11 we read: "The miry places thereof and the marshes thereof shall not be healed; they shall be given to salt." The miry places may fitly resemble sensual men. They have miry hearts; they are like the marshes that are not healed by the waters of the sanctuary. The Word of God does little good to sensual people.

REASON 4. Those who live according to sense live without God in the world. They give themselves up to lusts with greediness. As for God and Deity, they do not mind Him. They are a people who live without God and without

The Great Evil of Walking by Sense

Christ. And they shall live and perish; their end is destruction. You know what the apostle says in Romans 8:13: "He that lives after the flesh shall die," that is, he shall perish eternally. It's a most dreadful text and I admire those men who are led according to sense in the course of their lives, how they can read that Scripture without horror of conscience. In verse 8: "So then they that are in the flesh cannot please God." It is called flesh because that sin is motivated so much by the sensitive part. And then in verse 13: "If ye live after the flesh ye shall die." Now to live after the flesh is to live after the sensitive pleasures that give content to the flesh, and those things that are suitable to the flesh.

Now how do most men act in the course of their lives? Nothing but flesh, and that which is suitable to the flesh—that is what they bless themselves in. They have more to give contentment to the flesh than others have. Take some men who have a good estate and live on their means. Are their lives better than others? The flesh indeed has more pleasures than others: They have finer houses, sweeter gardens, or softer clothes. And then the appetite is more pleased: They have better food, and can eat and drink more delicately than others, which they account to be their happiness. Here is a man who lives by sense, but he is likely to perish forever. If you come to know no higher good, and you do not mind in the way of your lives any higher end than that which is according to sense, you are those who shall perish eternally. Indeed, the walk of sense is very pleasant, but it's a dangerous walk; and the end of it certainly will be death. Oh, that you would consider this and be humbled for walking according to the sight of your eyes.

Look back to the vanity of your youths; for young people usually walk so. Oh, look back; get alone and examine your hearts and lives and ask, "Why, Lord, am I not touched by this Word? Did it not concern me?" I find that men of the world walk according to sense, and that which is pleasant to sense. O Lord, it has been my way for a great part of my life. And any of you who do thus walk to this day, oh, that the Lord would smite you that you might come to see the evil of walking according to the sight of your eyes. Your eyes will be opened one day to see the evil of it, if they are not now.

It is no marvel that the Word does so little good to many people, when they walk according to the sight of the eyes, according to sense. Lay to your heart that Scripture that was named in Ecclesiastes 11:9: If your heart is set according to the eyes, "God will bring thee to judgement." For all those pleasant things that have delighted your senses in the course of your life, the Lord will bring you to judgement. That man or woman who has had the greater pleasure to sense shall have the greater account to give to the Lord. You must give account of all your sweet morsels and of all your stolen waters one day. Therefore be careful now to give way no further to your sense than that you may be able to give a comfortable account of it, if you were called before the Lord while this book is in your hand and you are reading it.

4

The Saints Do Not Walk by Sense

But though you walk thus, yet the saints do not. They do not judge things according to what they see with their eyes, nor according to what they feel. But they judge as Christ judged, for the saints certainly acted by Christ's spirit. See what the Spirit of Jesus Christ is in Isaiah 11:2, where it says that "the spirit of the Lord shall rest upon him, the spirit of wisdom and understanding, the spirit of counsel and might, the spirit of knowledge and of the fear of the LORD." Here's the Spirit of the saints, for they have a measure of the Spirit of Christ, which "shall make him of quick understanding in the fear of the LORD: and he shall not judge after the sight of the eyes, neither reprove after the hearing of his ears" (verse 3). He shall not be carried according to what appears to sense, "But with righteousness shall he judge the poor and reprove with equity for the meek of the earth: and he shall smite the earth with the rod of his mouth" (verse 4). If He should judge after the sight of His eyes then those who are poor people He would despise; those who are meek ones and put up wrongs He would not regard. What's the reason that people who are mean and poor, though never so godly, are despised by those who are carnal? It is because they judge by the sight of the eyes.

But the text says, "Christ shall not judge by the sight of His eyes." How then will He judge? With righteousness shall He judge the poor, and reprove with equity for the meek. He shall esteem them as high and honorable as the greatest and mightiest men in the world. You see how this was fulfilled in Matthew 5 when Christ came to show who were blessed. He begins thus: "Blessed are the poor" and the meek and the mourners. If Christ had judged by the sight of the eyes, He would never have judged so. I make no question but He means those who are outwardly poor and yet have a Spirit to glorify God in that poor condition, for you shall find in Luke 6 this sermon again. Christ does not say "poor in spirit," but "blessed are ye poor." He saw that the disciples were to suffer much afflictions and to be poor; therefore in preparing them for that He says, "Blessed are ye poor," that is, though you are poor in this world, yet, having hearts willing to submit to God and to honor God in that poor condition, "Blessed are ye poor." You are more blessed than if you had the greatest honor and riches in the world. He did not judge by the sight of His eyes. So Christians who are baptized with Christ's Spirit walk as Christ walked.

Therefore you find Job professing how far he was from being acted by sight in this way in Job 31:7-8: "If my step hath turned out of the way, and my mine heart walked after mine eyes...Then let me sow and another reap." And in the beginning of the chapter there he professed that he had made a covenant with his eyes. Oh, it's a notable Scripture. He made a covenant with his eyes and his heart did not walk after his eyes; but mark verse 2: "For what portion of God is there from above?" and "What inheritance of the Almighty from on high?" This Scripture, if God would but transcribe it on our spirits, might be a means of a great deal of good. I verily am persuaded that, though some may be more grossly than others, there is never one in this place but are very guilty of the evil of following the sight of their eyes. An abundance of sin, as you have read already, has been let in by the sight of the eyes.

Now look to it. Do not think it's a light matter, though perhaps you think, "Oh, God forbid that I should commit such an act of sin as the sight of my eyes does on occasions. No, I hope I am far from that." But mark what Job says, "For what portion of God is there from above?" and "What inheritance of the Almighty from on high?" It's as if he should say, "Lord, if I did give liberty to this, I was in danger never to have any portion from Thee, nor ever have any inheritance from the most High." And why does it give you so much contentment to wander after the sight of your eyes, that you will venture your portion in the Almighty and lose your inheritance in the Most High, never to have any good in Him? This would be a desperate thing, and yet truly so you do. Those men and women who follow the sight of their eyes, I say, so they do. And if there was no other sin but this, this would be enough to deprive you of God forever so that you should never have any portion in Him.

Oh, learn from this Scripture to do as Job did and make a covenant. It is no marvel that he made a covenant, for he speaks as if so be he should express himself thus: "I indeed have been convinced divers times that to follow the sight of my eyes is a dangerous evil, yet I find my heart would be working that way until I was glad to come to a peremptory resolution that I would not (the Lord assisting me) do so and to make a covenant, for I see I am undone otherwise." Oh, that God would cause this thought to stick in the heart of some man or woman to conclude with themselves: "Indeed, I confess my conscience tells me that my eyes have let in a great deal of evil to me, and I have thought that I would not take that liberty as formerly I have done. But now I see I am a lost soul forever unless I am more careful of the sight of my eyes."

When Job was in his greatest afflictions, one would have thought that if at any time his conscience would have stirred and accused him for walking after the sight of his eyes it would have been now. No, but in his greatest afflictions, and when his friends charged him of so great evils that he was guilty of because they walked according to the sight of their eyes, he could say, "If my step has turned out of the way and my heart walk after my eyes, oh, that you could but say so, and that you would be now so careful of the sight of your eyes that when you shall lie upon your dying pillow you may be able to appeal to God, and say 'Lord, Thou knowest I have not walked according to the sight of my eyes.' "

You see, then, that the saints do not walk according to the sight of their eyes, nor according to sense. No, they have mortified the flesh and crucified the lusts of it. The work of grace consists in mortifying the flesh and beating down the body. So David said in Psalm 119:37, Lord, "Turn away mine eyes from beholding vanity." This is a very excellent Scripture, and you would do well to take David's prayer and this one petition to God daily: "Turn away mine eyes from beholding vanity and quicken Thou me in thy way" (Psalm 119:37). David would gladly walk with God, but still he said, "Lord, when I am in the way walking with Thee, I find this hinders me very much. Lord, my eyes will be wandering after vanity, and I am dull in Thy way. Lord, turn away my eyes from beholding vanity." David was careful not so much as to look at vanity; and there's many who have their consciences so far convinced that they will not follow vanity. Yes, but they do not make conscience of having their eyes turned away from vanity. This holy man was necessitated to pray to God, and without God's help you will not be able to do this, for the eye is a quick thing. "O Lord, turn away mine eyes from vanity and quicken me in Thy way." It's as if he should say, "O Lord, it's this that makes me so dull that I cannot walk with Thee."

You have sometimes wondered to yourselves, "What a dead heart I have in the ways of God, though God has convinced me of the excellence of them and I have had some sense of the sweetness and goodness of them heretofore; but Lord, what's the matter? Do you ask "What's the matter?" Truly I hope God will tell you this, what it is, that your eyes run after vanity. It may be not after filthiness and uncleanness, as the eyes of some, but vanity. You have given liberty to your eyes to look after vanity, to the eyes of your body and the thoughts after this idle thing and the other vain thing. This is enough to deaden your hearts in that which is good, and you will never have a quick and lively spirit in that which is good until you come to make conscience of looking after vanity. Therefore, pray to God to turn your eyes away from beholding vanity so that you may be quicker in the Law of God, in the ways of holiness.

And you know what a charge our Savior gives: "If thy right eye offend thee, pluck it out." Our Saviour expresses the right eye to show that men may be carried many times by the eye to things that are evil, and it's very pleasing to the eye. But although it is your eye that is set upon things never so dear, it is better to be without your eye than to suffer your eye to run after that which is vanity. Not that he should pluck out his bodily eye, that's not the meaning, but get out the corruption of the eye, and so far as to account it a better thing to be without the eye. It would be better for many men and women to be blind rather than that they should give so much liberty to their eyes to look after such vanities as indeed they do. Though Christ would not have us to lay violent hands upon ourselves, yet He so speaks that we should be very careful, though we get never such satisfaction by it; and though it is very dear to us, yet we ought to labor to pluck out the corruption of our eyes. A godly man, we see, therefore does not walk according to the sight of his eyes.

Further, though things seem to the eye to go never so cross, yet a godly man does not alter his way. It's as if Paul had said, "I confess, if we should walk according to what we see in the world, we would never hold our course of Christianity. We see the promises are not fulfilled, but quite the contrary; we see the ways of God as they appear to the eye to be quite contrary to what He has said in the Word." Now we would be confused if we should look according to what we see with our eyes only, for we see that the most precious saints of God are persecuted and hated while the wicked and ungodly prosper. But should we go according to the sight of our eyes? Oh no, let us see the wicked prosper never so much, and the godly afflicted and persecuted, it's all one to us; we go on in our way. Oh, it's this that keeps the hearts of the saints close to God and His ways. Therefore, if you would keep close and deliver yourselves from temptations, consider seriously from this, and blessed be he who can believe though he does not see.

But many do not have such power of faith as to get beyond the eyes. Surely that faith that cannot get beyond sense is a poor and weak faith. There is not that preciousness in your faith as the Scriptures speaks of if it cannot overcome the eyes.

Furthermore, we walk by faith and not by sense for we by our senses do not apprehend those great things that take our hearts most. We cannot by our eyes see God; we

The Saints Do Not Walk by Sense

may see some works of His indeed, but we cannot see those mansions that are prepared for us. We cannot see Jesus Christ our Saviour, our Husband, our Head; and we cannot see those crowns of glory. We do not walk by sight, but because we cannot see those spiritual things we are not discouraged in our way. Even though God and Christ and heaven and those mansions and crowns of glory are not objects of our eyes, yet we go on in our way for all this.

"Yes," says a carnal heart, "if we could see these things. You speak of heaven, but can you see any thing beyond the sun moon and stars? You speak of the place of the blessed, but who ever saw it? You speak of mansions and crowns of glory, but who ever saw them?"

Now because they cannot be seen, therefore carnal hearts do not regard them. Yes, but though our eyes cannot act upon spiritual things, yet we go on in our way. You know how the people of Israel came to Moses and said, "Make us gods that may go before us." They would have something that they might see. Now, he says, we do not walk according to the sight of our eyes. Though we cannot see God, yet we believe in Him; though we cannot see Christ, yet we love Him; though we cannot see those mansions, yet we believe them and they are real to our faith, even though we have no sense of them. For example, God promises great things, yet many times we do not have the sense of God's love, and we do not have the sense of those spiritual things that God has promised. We do not feel them in our hearts.

But sometimes God refreshes us with the sense of His love, and sometimes our eyes are even open, as Stephen, who saw Christ at the right hand of the Father; while at other times, in regard to spiritual sense, we are in darkness, and God seems to appear against us as an enemy.

Now if we had nothing to walk by but by sight, what would we do? We find sometimes that God seems to come against us, and in our souls we find mighty griefs, sorrows, and troubles, and the joys of God are gone from us. Now we would be undone if we walked according to sense, but we have the help of our faith when all sense and sight fails.

I mention this now because we shall ground much upon it when we come to show how the saints walk by faith. When they lack sense—not only outward sense to encourage them, but an inward sense of the love and favor of God—yet then they walk by faith. It's true the men of the world do not know anything but by outward senses. When they are afflicted and feel pain in their bodies, then they feel by sense that which is very grievous to them. But the saints are afflicted in their senses with spiritual things, that is, they feel the want of God's love and of mercy and sweetness; they feel the want of the presence of God. And yet we go on; we have not only help to ourselves when the things to our bodies seem to be cross. It's true, indeed, that godliness has the promise of this life and of that which is to come, but we find according to our senses otherwise. Well, faith will help there, and we walk by faith.

And then to the sense of our souls, in respect of the loss of God's presence, that's more grievous, and the sadness of our spirits comes that way. Oh, the dark days that we have when we lose all sight there; yet there faith comes in and helps too, for we walk by faith and not by sight.

Here I shall show by many examples how the saints have not walked by sight in respect of spiritual things.

Consider Abraham. When God made those two great promises to him, that He would give him the land of Canaan and make his seed as the stars of heaven, if he had walked by sense it would have been ill with him, but it was

The Saints Do Not Walk by Sense

by faith. Now, if after these two promises were made he had walked by sight or sense, he would have been in an ill case; for the first thing that we read of Abraham after God had made that promise to him was that Abraham, as soon as he went into the land of Canaan, was ready to starve, and was forced to fly into the land of Egypt. This was to keep himself from starving, and yet this was the land that should flow with milk and honey, as a motive to him to forsake his father's house and kindred. Yes, but Abraham had faith to help him here. As for the other promise, that He would make his sees as the stars of heaven, Abraham, after this promise was made to him, waited twenty years and never had a child. Now if he had walked by sight, what would have become of him, both he and his wife having grown old? And after Isaac was born, who was the only son of the promise, yet Isaac must be sacrificed. If he had had no other principle but sense, what would have become of him? But he did not walk by sense. And Isaac waited forty years before he married, and he was another forty years without a child.

And so I might instance David, who had the promise of a kingdom and was accounted to be the King of Israel. The next thing you read of David is that Saul, the king, persecuted him to take away his life. He was hunted up and down like a partridge in the wilderness. Then, at one time sense began to prevail with David: "One day I shall perish by the hand of Saul," and "in my haste I did say all men are liars," that the prophets and all were liars. Oh, but it was spoken in his haste. Sense prevailed now and faith seemed to be dead. But at other times you shall see his faith exceedingly strong. He walked by faith not by sight.

I shall show more afterwards when we come to the excellence of the walk of faith. And if you read Psalm 88 of Heman, who was a godly man, yet he had that which was contrary to sense all his days; if he had walked according to sense, he would have been the most miserable man that could be. He suffered the terrors of God from his youth up, and he was even distracted again. When he gave but a little way to sense, yet the Lord carried him on.

And so I might hint to you many Scriptures where the Church was afflicted and tossed up and down, so that if it should have gone according to sense it would have been undone. Oh, the very naming of these things to you will show the necessity and excellence of the point of walking by faith and not by sense. Now this the Lord would have His servants do because the more spiritual sense they have, the less faith they have ordinarily; and faith does not appear in the acts of it when there is so much spiritual sense. We would gladly have sense, and it is a lovely and excellent thing, but God sees that, for the most part, when we have the most sense we have the less faith, and so we are ready to rest upon sense.

Observe this one thing: There is nothing more in God's design while we live here upon the earth than the advancing of His glory in the work of faith—although God has His glory in the exercise of all grace, yet above all in the exercise of faith. We would gladly give God the glory by our enlargements in prayer, by our joy, by going on cheerfully in the course of lives, and by prospering in our way and carrying on all business before us. Yes, if always the Church might prosper and her enemies be down, the saints might live joyfully, and all things that they undertake they might carry before them without any contradiction, you would think God's glory would be set out that way.

Oh, you are childish and foolish to think so. "No," God says, "rather let Me hide Myself and the saints be in want of My presence, then will they act in faith; the naked acts of faith will then appear." Faith will then appear in its own proper virtue. It's as if God should say, "I do not see faith in its own genuine and proper virtue when there is sense joined with it. How does it appear that these live by faith rather than sense when they have such encouragements by sense? No, I will therefore take away these things for this end, that I may have My Name glorified by the works of faith."

And this I verily believe is the cause of the sad conditions of the saints in this world, and why things go so cross: The saints are persecuted and the wicked prevail in their designs. It is upon this ground, that God may advance faith, from the infinite delight that God has in the grace of faith rather than in other graces. And this because it is a grace that God shall have the glory of in this life only, for it will cease in time to come. Now God, having the glory of this only in this world, therefore it is that He will put them much to the acting of it, which will be discovered more when we come to show the walking of the saints by faith.

5

An Admonition to Young Converts

If this is the walk of the saints not walking by sense, I beseech you, you who are young converts to whom God gives sense for the present, lay this truth up; you will have use of it if you live. It is common when God converts the soul at first that He encourages it by the sense of His love, with an abundance of sense and joy. Yes, but they do not have as much faith as others have less sense afterwards. But if you are not careful you will be ready to rest upon this sense of joy and to think that according to the increase of it, so is the increase of grace; and accordingly the decrease of it is a decrease of grace. Yes, but you judge as children in this. Oh, therefore, take this caveat, you who are beginning in the ways of God and have sense. Oh, lay up for a rainy day. It's not the way of God to bring the saints to heaven the way of sense, no, but by the way of faith. You think through God's mercy I have some sense of His love; yes, but this may not always be. Alas, these are but like bladders that you make use of when you would teach a young swimmer. He must not expect to have his bladder always. Afterwards, when he is a little exercised, he who taught him will take away his bladder and leave him without them. Then he scrabbles and gets up, and afterwards he can tread the water and swims better without them than with them.

Just so at first God does, as it were, put sense underneath to uphold His people, even like the bladder does the one learning to swim. God has His time to take away these bladders, and you shall have nothing in the world to live upon but faith. And if God enables you to live by faith it will be a better life than the other one was. It is in this case as it is in the work of nature. When children are first born, they grow mightily for a time; you shall have a child who is born but a month ago who shoots up very much, but after it comes to more maturity it does not shoot up so much in so little a time. Now this reason may be given: The child comes out of the mother's womb, where it lay hot and warm, and comes into to the air where it's colder, and unless nature puts itself forth very much the child would not be able to live. That may be one reason.

And so it is in the work of grace. When God makes a change in the heart, at first there's a great deal of opposition and the saints are but weak; therefore God, to help and strengthen them, gives them sense. Afterwards, when they come to riper years and grow to a better understanding in the ways of God, they shall not think to shoot up so high in so little a time, that is, so sensible as others may perceive it. Thus the Lord supplies according to our necessities both in nature and in grace; and therefore let this be laid up. Oh, you who have sense at any time, do not think that you must always be so; do not think that God will always dandle you, as it were, upon His knee. At first you dandle your children upon your knee, but afterwards you will put them in to school and cause them to wait upon you at your table. But this is not because you love them less afterwards than you did before, no, but because as they grow up they must live by other principles. They live by sense at first, and therefore you only please their senses; but as they grow up they come to have a harder kind of life. And so it is with God's children. Though the Lord dandles them at first and they live rather by sense, though spiritual sense, yet as they grow up more and more they come to live harder and harder because the Lord would have them to exercise faith.

Consider this and make use of it; you who are Christians find the need of it in the course of your lives.

The principle that the saints have is beyond the sight of reason, and that I am likewise to speak to in the same manner as to the former.

First, it is beyond the sight of natural reason.

Second, it is beyond spiritual reason. The saints are so far from resting upon things that are suitable to natural reason, and from being guided by that, as they are beyond even spiritual and that which is sanctified knowledge. Faith is beyond that.

6

Worldly Men Walk According to What They Apprehend to Be Reason

Indeed, the men of the world, those who are in their natural estate, their walk is according to their eyes, according to what they apprehend by reason.

The happiness and highest good that they have is but that which in a way of reason they apprehend and no higher; and therefore it is but natural reason.

Their course and way is but according to what principle of reason they have. If there is any thing propounded to them in the walk with God that is not suitable to their natural reason, they reject it. A man's natural reason, if it is but guided by the rules of it, may help him to converse with men very much in the ways of justice between man and man. But when he comes to deal with God in matters of eternal estate and of divine worship, there let him look to himself that he is not acted by his reason for he will be undone if he is.

Therefore, first, I shall show you how carnal hearts are acted by reason in the course of their lives, and especially in the way of God's worship; second, how this is not a good rule to walk by; third, the danger that there is in walking according to the rules of men's reason; and then I shall apply it. Then later I will treat the matter of sanctified knowledge.

I find five notable expressions of carnal hearts to show how they are acted by their own reason.

They lean to their own understanding. In Proverbs 3:5 there's a caution: "Lean not to thine own understanding," noting that men naturally do lean to their own understanding. It's that which supports them and props them up. Let them come and hear from the Word things that are against them, yet they lean to their own understanding and regard that rather than the Word. Hosea 13:2 speaks of this sort of worship of God: "And now they sin more and more, and have made them molten images of their silver, and idols according to their own understanding." They had a way of God's worship set out unto them in the Word, but that would not serve them; they must go according to their own understandings. Oh, this has been the way of carnal men's worshipping of God in all ages! What kind of worship and service of God have we had of late but that which is according to men's own understanding? And therefore we used to say, "I think this is very good, and there's no hurt in such and such things, for they are very decent and comely." Yes, but that's according to your own understandings, which should not be the way of God's worship, for this should be according to God's Word. Hereupon general counsels and synods have seldom been successful about the matter of God's worship, because men came with confidence, leaning on their own understandings. That's the first phrase, when men go according to their own understanding.

According to the imagination of their own hearts. This you have in Jeremiah 9:14. Oh, they would rather walk according to their own hearts than according to what is revealed unto them by the Word.

Walking according to their own counsels. They would rather walk according to the plots, imaginations, and counsels of men's minds than to follow the counsel of the Word. And that you have in Psalm 81:12: "They walked in their own counsels," and, indeed, God in judgement gave them up to their own counsels.

According to their own thoughts. Isaiah 65:2 is a very remarkable Scripture for this. The reason for the wickedness of men, and why they resisted all the offers of grace and the invitations of Christ was this: "Because they did walk according to their own thoughts. I have spread out My hands unto a rebellious people." Here God complains that all the day long He has spread out His hands, but to whom? "To a rebellious people." But how did they come to be so rebellious and not profit by God spreading out His hands? As a man, when he is earnest about a thing, spreads out his hands to embrace another, so God in the offers of grace spreads out His hands ready to embrace wretched sinners. But they are rebels for all this, and the reason for this comes in the next words of the text: "Which walketh in a way that was not good." And what way was that but, "after their own thoughts." Oh, lay up this Scripture and remember it; take heed of walking in a way after your own thoughts.

You think it's a good way, but the way after your own thoughts is an evil way, a rebellious way; it's that which makes you to be rebels against God. How many men and women are there, when they have some truths darted into their spirits that begin to show unto them that the way that they have walked in heretofore has not been good? Then they begin to think thus: "If I change this way, I shall have a deal of trouble in it and shall lose this and the other, and it will not be comfortable for me." And so, according to their own thoughts, they will order their way. Oh, this is a dangerous way to walk, to walk in a way according to your own thoughts. I beseech you, poor soul, take heed of your thoughts, for there's nothing more dangerous to undo you than your own thoughts. And this is because they are so near to men that they let them in and dandle their own thoughts; but those thoughts that you please yourself with many times in are the thoughts that are likely to undo you forever. They walk according to their own thoughts.

They are wise in their own eyes, as you have it in Isaiah 5:21, and so in many different places in Proverbs. This is to walk by sight, to walk according to the apprehensions of men's own reason; but the apostle did not, nor dare walk so. This is one main thing in the walking according to sight and reason, that is, such as are led according to what they see, working in a natural way, by natural causes. A man who lives by the candle light of reason looks no further than second causes. If he sees second causes working thus and thus, then he will go that way and follow the tract of second causes. Now, certainly, so long as your soul is tied unto a tract of second causes, to work according to them, you are not acquainted with the spiritualness of the ways of God, or with this walk of faith. Therefore, reason is not that which should guide us in our way.

7

Reason Is Not That Which Should Guide a Christian

Reason is too low a thing to be the guide of a Christian. It is inferior to the happiness that God made man for. God has higher thoughts about man, to bring him to a higher happiness than reason can reach unto. The outward senses are too low to guide a man who would live like a rational creature; they are not enough to guide men in a civil way. So reason is too low a thing to guide men in a way that must lead to that supernatural happiness that God has made the children of men for. Take reason, though not corrupted reason, but right reason; for I do not speak of reason as it is corrupted. Suppose man's reason was not corrupted at all, but merely ordered according to what is right reason. Still it would be too low to bring you to that glorious state that God made man for. Yes, if your reason was as perfect as Adam's was in Paradise, yet it would be too low; for the first man was of the earth, earthly, and his happiness was a kind of earthly happiness. But that which God has made man for now is a higher happiness.

But it is too low especially if we consider how it is corrupted. If our reason had not received a blow, but was as perfect as Adam's was in innocence, and understood God and the mind of God as Adam did, yet this could not bring us to that happiness that God has made man for. The way of the gospel is higher than Adam understood, higher than his reason was capable of.

But our reason is corrupted, and the Scriptures tell us of the wisdom of the flesh, that it is enmity with God. The apostle in Romans 8 not only says that wisdom, the higher part of flesh, is an enemy, but enmity to God. So the carnal mind, or wisdom of the flesh, "is enmity to God, for it is not subject to the Law of God, neither indeed can it be." Mark the opposition, it is enmity, for it is not subject to the law of God, nether can be. Oh, what an opposition is here! And so you have another Scripture in the Epistle to the Colossians, where the apostle speaks of the state of the Gentiles and what they were before they were converted to God. There he tells you "that we were enemies in our minds by wicked works." In your mind, that is, your very reason was so corrupted as it was nothing but enmity against God. The apprehensive and discursive part of reason is opposite to God and therefore in 1 John 5:20 it is said that God has given us understanding, a mind to know Him. The word signifies the discursive faculty, discourse of the mind and reason, whereby we may come to know the things of God. The very discourses of men, as they are natural, are corrupted. The Lord sees the thoughts of the wise to be but vain and corrupt, and therefore you know what our Savior said: "I thank Thee, O Father, Lord of heaven and earth, that Thou hast hid these things from the wise and prudent." And so says the apostle: "Not many wise, not many rich, not many mighty."

And here I shall show you, first, the corrupt principles that reason carries men upon, and, second, how reason is opposite and contrary to those main spiritual truths that should carry men on in the way to life.

8

Reason Carries Men Upon Corrupt Principles

How men who are guided by reason; are carried on by corrupt principles:

1. It is not good for a man to engage himself too far in any cause. Men who are wise for themselves and are carried on by the wisdom of the flesh are acted by this corrupt principle, that it is not good to be engaged in anything too far. There may be more danger in such a thing than I am aware of, therefore let me go on fair and softly and not engage myself too far. This is one principle of corrupt reason, and I verily believe that as I am naming them, many may go along with me and have cause to lay their hands upon their hearts and say, "The Lord be merciful to me. Thus I have walked by sight, according to reason, even these corrupt principles that have in this book been mentioned before me.

2. It is not good to cross the stream and course of the tide where I live; it's the safest way for us to go according to the common streams of the times and places where we live. This is that which the apostle in Ephesians 2 says was the way of men while they were in their natural state: "In times past you walked." How? "According to the course of this world." That was your walk; you saw the course of the world, how it was, and you thought in reason it was fit to go according to the current. That's the principle that acts

many politicians who are accounted the wise men of the world; they are spirited by this principle.

3. Corrupt reason says not to venture present things for future ones, and certain things for uncertain things. Men who are wise according to the flesh will not venture things that are present for things to come, especially looking upon things that are present as certain, and the other they imagine to be uncertain. Now upon this principle they are so acted and guided in their course that it makes them put off the things of God; for the special and chief things of God are things that are future and by reason they can never be made certain. In Hebrews 11 it says "Faith is the evidence of things not seen." Now according to the principle of reason it seems to be a foolish thing for men to venture a certain good for that which is to come, and for I know not what and I know not when. This is against reason, and it's that which makes the wise of the world to go on in their way and to embrace this present world, as is said of Demas. It seems he was wise for himself, for Paul told him of things that were to come hereafter, but he forsook him and embraced this present world.

4. It's not likely that a poor, contemptible man should come to understand more than the learned rabbis and grandees of the world. Would reason think that a few poor men who are condemned in the world, and whose parts of nature are but very low in all earthly things, yet that these should be the men who would come to understand the mind of God more than men who are learned and wise in the learning of the Egyptians, who had better breeding and education? A man thinking reasonably could never imagine this; and this is the great stumbling block to men of the world. They look and see who are they who go on in such ways, not the scribes and Pharisees,

not the rulers of the people, but the multitude. Now is this likely to be the right way? Reason would tell one that 'tis not likely to be the right way. Reason would inform one that the other way was more likely to be the right way. Oh, it would be a mercy of God for men to be delivered from this corrupt principle of reason.

5. To be happy, poor, and persecuted are inconsistent. Carnal men walk by their sight and by their reason. Thus for one to be happy and yet to be poor and contemptible in the world, to be persecuted and yet to be the happiest in the earth, is that which reason cannot comprehend, and therefore, according to that principle they walk. They cannot believe happiness, persecution, poverty, contempt, and scorn can consist together; this is a riddle, a paradox to them. And yet you shall observe that when the Lord Christ, who is the wisdom of the Father, and knows fully the mind of the Father, when He comes to teach us wherein blessedness consists He begins with poverty and ends with persecution. Read Matthew 5 and see how He begins: "Blessed are the poor." And in Luke 6 He leaves out poor in spirit and ends with this: "Blessed are ye when ye are persecuted for righteousness sake."

6. Good meanings and performances of good duties are sufficient to make one acceptable to God. A man in reason cannot imagine what people mean to take men off from duties and that their good meanings are not sufficient. They wonder that their good hearts and meanings, that good works and performance of holy duties, living fairly and civilly, that the performance of these things should not make them acceptable to God. They cannot compass this; this is a corrupt principle that many go by.

7. The zeal and forwardness that there is in some beyond others must come from the hypocrite. Men act

merely by reason because they do not understand those spiritual principles that godly people are led by. They cannot judge in reason what need there is in some kind of men. The wise men of the world walk according to such principles.

9

Spiritual Truths Are Above the Light of Natural Reason

There are other things that are very much above the light of men's reason:

1. The necessity of a new birth, of regeneration; that a man must not only be better than he was, but that he must be born again. You know in John 3, the story of Nicodemus, that man of great parts and understanding, a ruler among the people, yet how childish was this man in the great principle of regeneration, for he said, "Must a man enter into his mother's womb and be born again? How can these things be?"

2. Then there is this great thing that is mightily above man's reason: The more a man prospers, if he is wicked, the more cursed he is. Reason cannot apprehend this; it is cross to it.

3. That God should work the worst of things that befall the saints for good unto them, though it is ever so cross and ill to them, is above the light of reason. That this should work for their good is a principle beyond reason and they cannot understand it: men who walk according to reason can never come to believe this.

4. The greatest riches that any man can have in the world consist in the promises. These principles are foolish things to such as walk by reason. The promises that are in the Word will make a man richer than all the gold and silver in the world. A man who is merely guided by reason

laughs at these things and thinks them but the mere silly conceits of men.

5. All the world is vanity; that's a foolish thing to one who is guided by reason. What! That all the pomp and glory of all the monarchs on earth is nothing but vanity! Come and preach of such things, that our riches are in the promises and all the world is but vanity, and such a one who walks by reason will slight and disregard it.

6. Another principle that he can have no skill in is this: We must be righteous by the righteousness of another, that nothing but a perfect righteousness, and that a righteousness out of ourselves must be there to present us as acceptable before God. This is beyond reason.

7. Another is this: The foundation of all happiness is self-denial and mortification. If a man would be happy, he must lay the foundation of his happiness in denying himself, in denying his will and his own thoughts, in the mortifying of the flesh, in especially opposing that sin he is most inclined to, and there he may lay the very groundwork of his happiness. This reason will not attain unto.

8. The last is this: There is greater evil in the least sin than there is in the greatest affliction. I have already demonstrated this out of that great point that I have long since treated, that the evil of the least sin is greater that the evil of the greatest affliction whatsoever [EDITOR'S NOTE: The author is referring to his book entitled *The Evil of Evils*], that it is a greater evil for a man to tell a lie or to have an unclean thought and give way to it than it is to suffer the loss of all his estate, than to have all that he has consumed by fire or water, than to have any evil that can be imagined to befall him. Now come and tell this to a man who has nothing but reason, who walks by the sight of his eyes, and he will treat these things with scorn and deri-

Spiritual Truths Are Above the Light of Reason

sion. And yet, truly, though many who do thus walk according to these principles do not own them and say that they walk thus. But God sees that they act by such things as these are, and for such principles as should carry them on in the way of eternal life; they are above them and they do not apprehend them. I affirm God knows it, and your consciences know it, and may tell you that you do not apprehend those principles that are higher than religion.

But those who walk by faith walk by these principles that are above reason; therefore you know what the Scripture says: "The natural man perceives not the things of God, neither can he, for they are spiritually discerned" (1 Corinthians 2:14). The natural man cannot receive them; they are but foolish and silly things to him. The phrase "natural man" in the text is the same word translated "sensual man" in Jude 9, that is, one who is carried on by his natural soul. As there is in man a sensitive soul, so there is in man a rational soul. The natural man here is one who is moved by his rational soul, and such a one as does not receive the things of the Spirit of God. The water rises no higher than the spring from whence it came; so natural men can ascend no higher than nature. Such a mere animal, such a sapless fellow we may read of in Psalm 14:1. He cannot receive them; they are foolishness to him because they are spiritually discerned. As I hinted before in the matter of sense, so here in reason, it is the design of God to advance faith above it and to beat down sense, to mortify the flesh. The danger in men walking according to reason follows.

10

The Danger of Men Walking by Reason

1. The way that God has set for your eternal life is a way that is above reason. It's a special design of God for to hoodwink the wisdom of the world and to take the wise in their own craftiness; this is what God aims at. If you read 1 Corinthians 1:17, and following, the apostle says: "Christ sent me not to baptize, but to preach the gospel; not with wisdom of words, lest the cross of Christ should be made of none effect." It is as if he had said, "It was Christ's charge that when I came to preach the gospel, I should not go in that plausible way of reason as others do, in a rhetorical and logical way, and to manifest art so much." It's true, there is use to be made of arts and sciences that may be understood by the light of nature, yet the way of the gospel must be that which is above them and it must be delivered in a way above the way of reason. Therefore, Paul says, "I came not with wisdom of words," which he could have done as well as others. Witness his artificial undoing of the orator's speech in Acts 16. But he did not like to put the Sword of the Spirit into a velvet scabbard so that it could not pierce, to speak as those self-seekers at Corinth did, who sought more to tickle the ear than to affect the heart, to please rather than to profit. Thus the apostle purposely waved all gaudy, court-like preaching "lest the cross of Christ should be made of none effect, for the preaching of the cross is to them that perish foolish-

The Danger of Men Walking by Reason

They see no wisdom in it, and then verse 19 says: "For it is written, I will destroy the wisdom of the wise and bring to nothing the understanding of the prudent." The way that God has to bring men to life and to salvation is to make them fools first in their own apprehensions, to convince them of the corruption that is there in their understandings. Then in verse 20 it is asked: "Where is the wise (the teacher of traditions)? Where is the scribe (the textman)? Where is the disputer of this world (the teacher of allegories and mysteries)? Hath not God made foolish the wisdom of this world?" And so he goes on: "For after that, in the wisdom of God (not by all their natural reason) it pleased God by the foolishness of preaching to save them that believe" (verse 21). "For the Jews require a sign and the Greeks seek after wisdom" (verse 22). "But we preach Christ crucified, unto the Jews a stumbling block, and unto the Greeks foolishness" (verse 23). "But unto them which are called, both Jews and Greeks, Christ is the power of God, and the wisdom of God" (verse 24).

Even Christ and the great things of the gospel are foolishness to those who walk according to the sight of reason, for, says Paul, "The foolishness of God is wiser than men" (verse 25). Here Paul speaks in the apprehension of the world, that is, the great things of God are accounted by men of the world but foolishness, yes, but it's wiser than their wisdom. And therefore you "see your calling brethren, how not many wise men after the flesh, not many mighty, not many noble are called. But God hath chosen the foolish things of the world to confound the wise; and God hath chosen the weak things of the world to confound the things that are mighty; and base things of the world, and things which are despised hath God chosen, yea, and things which are not (that are nought set by) to bring to nought things that are" (verses 26–28).

You may see by this Scripture how God's design is to blast the wisdom of this world and to hoodwink all worldly excellencies. He has so set things in the way of salvation that those who will stick according to the rules of their own reason must perish and be undone eternally. They shall never come to know the things of God.

2. It is a dangerous thing further (yet reason, considered without the corruption of it, is an excellent thing) because walking according to it turns that which is an excellent thing in itself to be a mischief to you. It is a means to harden you against God and His ways, and to be a means to put off the truths. A man who has strong natural parts, deep reason, and yet a corrupt heart, oh, how can this man fence the truth of God when others cannot. Hence it is that many times the Word works upon those who are weaker in natural parts than upon others because when the Word of God comes to such a one, he has nothing to fence off the truth, whereas another man who is subtle, and has strong natural parts, will have this and the other objections against it. Surely this cannot be so because of this reason and the other reason; and so he seems to impede the truths of God when indeed he does but check his own soul. And so he blesses himself that he has baffled it and fenced it off, whereas it is but for his own ruin.

When Christ came to preach, where do you read of Christ converting any scribes and Pharisees, who were the learned men of the times? You read of Paul, who was a long time in Athens, yet you never read that there was a church set up in Athens—but there was a church set up at Ephesus, at Galatia, at Colossae, and at Philippi. Now at

The Danger of Men Walking by Reason

Athens was the university; it was the place where the scholars and learned men were, and they derided Paul and jeered at him. And so the Pharisees derided Christ because they, by the strength of their parts, could put off the truths of God. Oh, it's a miracle to see a man who has strong natural parts and a corrupt heart converted. Of all men, if God converts them, they have cause to bless God abundantly. Oh, they will then see how their natural parts were opposed to the work of conversion, and will stand and wonder how God overpowered their objecting hearts.

3. And, by the way, you who have weak natural parts, do not be discouraged, for perhaps if you had had greater natural parts you might never have come to the understanding of spiritual things as now you have. You read in Scripture of the women who followed Christ and His apostles; and when as Paul was sent to preach in Macedonia and he had a vision in the night, saying, "Come over to Macedonia and help us," we find that there were but few women who came to hear Paul, and among the rest God opened the heart of one Lydia, a seller of purple. Men of strong natural parts fence off the truths and keep them at arm's end; but men of weaker parts have received them. And now this will be the glory of God to all eternity when you come to heaven, that God should chose you to reveal Himself to rather than the great ones of the world. And therefore do not be discouraged for the weakness of your natural parts. There's a great deal of danger in walking according to the sight of men's knowledge and reason.

4. Again, there is this further evil in it: It makes men very slight in Scriptural duties. Men who have nothing but reason will perform duties, but there's no life, no vigor at all, no warmth of their hearts and no communion with God in them. I appeal to your consciences, many of you

who have gone but merely in a fair rational way before the world, though you pray and come to the Word, I ask you what communion with God do you have? Those who walk according to sight and reason are far from enjoying communion with God. Their hearts are very slight and dead in things that are spiritual and heavenly. All the services that they perform are merely natural, and therefore in a very low and mean way they do them. Then you shall find those who are far beneath them in natural parts, when they come to pray, oh, there's a spiritualness and heavenliness in their prayers; and you shall have many poor people of very weak parts sending up groans and sighs in prayer. But to some who are scholars, who will have fine quaint prayers and set phrases, yet they have no warmth at all, no heat, no spiritualness at all in them, because they go according to reason and act no higher than the mere principles of reason.

5. Moreover, those who go according to the principles of reason may make an outlet upon some work that God sets them about, but, a thousand to one, they will never go through it. If there comes any difficulty in the way, they will quickly be carried off. There is no way to persevere in godliness but by being principled merely by a principle of faith. If the principle is merely by a principle of reason, you will never go through a duty; but you will falter in it when you meet with any difficulty, or start aside like a broken bow.

6. Again, there is this evil in it: If ever God works grace upon any, they will be more full of doubts and fears and perplexities than others are; ordinarily it is so. There is this evil in the remainder of corrupt reason, and I have seen it by the examples that I have known of many men of excellent parts. They, being converted, have had more doubts

The Danger of Men Walking by Reason

about the mystery of religion, more troubled with thoughts of atheism, more perplexed in many things, and more followed with fears about their own estates. They, having been so addicted unto reason, there remain so much strength of it after their conversion as their reason puzzles them extremely. Whereas you have many of the meaner sort of people, when God works sanctifying grace in their hearts, they never have any such doubts and fears. They look at nothing, but in the morning commit their souls to God and read the Word. And when they meet with a promise their souls close with it and bless God for it. And they so bless God for it that they go about their business with comfort and joy, and never call anything into question.

The devil does not have a forge in their understandings fit for his turn. But certainly a man's understanding that is of a large capacity, and not perfectly sanctified, the devil can make a great use of the unsanctified part of it to forge a great many questions and doubts that will puzzle and perplex the soul. So far as you walk according to reason, so far you will be brought into perplexity. And therefore there is a great deal of danger in walking according to the sight of the eyes.

Now we move to the application.

11

The Application of the Doctrine

Hence you see what a vain thing it is to follow the examples of men of parts.

USE 1. If it is so evil to walk according to the sight of men's understanding, then surely it's a vain thing to walk as they walk and to make their walk to be the rule of your walk. Oh, no, we must not walk according to our own reason, much less according to the reason of other men—that's a double folly. It's a folly and danger to walk according to the dictates of our own reason, and to walk according to other men's is a very great madness. No, we should seek that God would open our eyes so that we may understand, and that by a principle higher than reason, so that we may walk in a safe way indeed.

USE 2. Let men who are gifted learn to be humbled before God. There's nothing in the world that puffs up men's minds more than the strength of abilities, than the quick sight that they have of things. When they come into company and see that they have insights beyond their companion, and can see into a business more clearly than others, they are ready to despise other men and they are somebody in their own thoughts. Oh, walk humbly before the Lord, you who have gifts more than others, lest your gifts be your undoing, lest God gives you up to walk according to your own understanding, unto your own counsels, and then you are undone.

USE 3. It's a use of special direction to those upon whom God begins at first to work the work of conversion, unto young converts. I beseech you to consider this one thing, and lay this up; and if God would but settle this one thing home, it may recompense you for what difficulties you come through to wait at wisdom's gate, that is, when God is beginning to make Himself known to you and to show you things of Jesus Christ and your eternal state. Take heed of poring too much by the eye of reason and judging things according to reason, for it will keep you off from Christ if you do so.

If you would indeed have the Word go on graciously and comfortably in your hearts, you must lay the naked Word and your hearts together, and do not puzzle yourselves by reason, such as when you reason, "I cannot understand how this and this thing should be thus and thus." Know that when God begins to work in a poor soul the devil casts in this temptation, and reason helps strengthen it. That such a poor wretch as I, so vile, so wicked, yet that God should reject them who are able to do great things, repeat sermons, and have great memories, and yet God should reject them and have regard to me. What service can I do for God? Surely it will never come to good. Yes, reason will tell you all this, and in a way of reason that you cannot see how this should be. But when you have to do in matters that concern your souls, you must remember not to be moved by the eye of your understanding; it is a dangerous thing.

I remember Luther had such a speech: "Reason is the most cruel enemy to faith that can be." And in another place he said, "In the matters of God we must not be asking why so, and what's the reason of everything?" If we walk according to reason in the great things of godliness and eternal life, we shall hinder ourselves exceedingly. Therefore, let all young converts, in matters that concern their souls and eternal states, not to hearken too much to what reason says. And though reason says it cannot be, yet know, if the Word says otherwise, I must go according to the Word. "I do not know how it could be, I cannot see how such a wretched heart as mine should ever be brought to any good at all and how God should take delight and pleasure in me, and how I should come to have communion with God, I cannot see how I could ever come to this." Well, though you cannot see it, look at the Word and rather shut the eye of reason than follow the dictates of reason. We must not walk by sight, nor walk by the eye of reason.

USE 4: Further, this should rebuke those who do not even come up so high as reason. There are many who walk in such a base and wicked course that reason would convince them to the contrary; and God will bring their reason against them one day. The Gentiles, who had nothing but the sight of reason, would have scorned such ways as many walk in; they would abominate those ways of yours. Then how far are you from the walk of the saints and walking with God who do not come to so high a walk as the very heathens walk. They walked up more to the rules of right reason than you do.

USE 5. The saints should be so far from ordering their ways according to reason, since their very sanctified knowledge is not sufficient. Though they come to have the Spirit of God to sanctify their reason, yet they must have a principle beyond this. I mean by this that sanctified knowledge is not sufficient. There are many things, and those the great and necessary things of eternal life, which are things that are to be apprehended by a principle beyond knowledge, which is faith that we cannot by knowledge come to apprehend. For example, the mystery of the Trinity, of the personal union of both natures of Christ, how these bodies of ours should come to be more glorious than the sun in the firmament. It's impossible that we should come by knowledge to have these things made real to us in this world; no, it must be by faith. The evidence that we have of them is not because we come to understand these things, how these things should be by any knowledge, but merely because we believe what God has said. That's the difference between taking things by faith and taking things by knowledge.

We do not say that we believe that two times two is four because we know it by reason, rather our believing is grounded upon the testimony of another, and the proper object of faith is such things as are out of reach of knowledge. I work upon some principles of knowledge, indeed, there are some principles that I know and I ground upon them whereby I come to know God says thus and thus. And then I come to have this made evident to me by faith that goes beyond knowledge. For those things that we apprehend by faith are such things that we shall have and enjoy when knowledge is gone. In 1 Corinthians 13 the apostle says, "We now see through a glass darkly; but then face to face; now I know in part, but then shall I know even as also I am known" (verse 12). Our sanctified knowledge is not that which shall be hereafter. But by faith we come to have the same things by effect, though not in degree, such as the things of heaven and eternal life that we shall enjoy when knowledge shall be done away. Faith can get into heaven to the throne of God and make evident and clear to the soul such things as we cannot come to have by knowledge, though our knowledge is sanctified.

Observe what I mean in it. If we had nothing but knowledge, and knowledge sanctified, that is, our understanding delivered from our corruption and made as perfect as Adam's was, yea, though our knowledge had some sanctified grace whereby we were able to understand many spiritual things beyond what Adam did, yet still there is something that we cannot have by sanctified knowledge without a higher principle. We cannot fetch in the truths of the Trinity, nor of the personal union of the two natures of Christ. Though our reasonings may have grace in them, yet there is something in the makeup of faith that is able to fetch in truth to be real to the soul; and that is what I think the apostle here meant, for he speaks how that when we are at home in the body, we are absent from the Lord. We know something of God now though we are in the body; yes, but we are absent from God for all that, for the apostle says, "We walk by faith, and not by sight." That is, there are other things of God we can see and understand by knowledge, yet by faith these are made real to us. Therefore, in Hebrews 11, it says that "faith is the evidence of things not seen." Certainly there the apostle does not mean by "things not seen" only things that I do not see with my bodily eyes, but it is the evidence of things that I cannot see with my understanding. Yea, I cannot see in a way of knowledge. Though my knowledge is sanctified to me, yet I cannot come by my knowledge to take in those things and make them evident to me, but by faith they are; so that we walk by faith and not by sight. Beyond all our knowledge and beyond all out sanctified knowledge, we have a principle that carries us higher.

12

Saints Can Expect Greater Glory Than They Understand

Certainly there are greater things that the saints by faith are taught to expect, and by faith are made evident to them, greater things than ever they knew or could reach to by any spiritual understanding. We can, by our spiritual understanding, come to know that there is a great good in communion and enjoyment of God; but faith makes good to us a greater good than we can know.

We have some notions about God and heaven, but faith is higher than all our knowledge; and therefore the saints may expect greater happiness and glory in heaven than ever they understood. The weakest Christian who has his understanding elevated by spiritual illumination is able to understand such things as the strongest man in the world who is ripest in his natural parts cannot reach unto. But you, by the exercise of your faith, may bring home to your soul the comfort of things beyond all your spiritual understanding, and so you may pray to God that He would do you good beyond what you can ask or think. Yes, this is the life indeed of a Christian, when a Christian not only makes use of natural understanding and rises as high as he can there, but when a Christian is illuminated by spiritual illumination and so comes to understand the things of God, and then comes with an act of faith. Yes, but there are things that are beyond all these things that I know. For knowledge is by the causes or by the effects, but faith goes beyond the taking in things by causes and effects; it takes in merely by revelation so that faith brings to the soul things that are unutterable. As Paul said of himself when he was caught up into the third heaven, there he heard words that were unutterable; and so faith raises the souls of men to converse with the things of heaven that are unutterable and inconceivable to their understanding. And this is the excellence of a Christian: When he can walk thus, he can walk on high. This is to walk with God.

Grace raises reason higher than it was, and takes away much corruption from reason. Yet the principle of the saints in their walks is beyond their sanctified reason. Thus the main thing that guides and carries the saints on in their way is that which is beyond what can be known by reason in this world, though elevated to the greatest height. For instance, the principle things of the Christian religion that the good of the saints consists in cannot be known by reason; though elevated by grace, it must be in a way of faith and believing. Such things as one God in three Persons we believe, but we cannot know that there is One in three, Father, Son, and Holy Spirit. Reason can never reach to this, even though it is sanctified. Likewise, that the way of salvation is by a Mediator, God and Man, is beyond reason in its greatest height. The glory of the body, that it should be made more glorious than the sun, the way of our communion with God and Christ in heaven, for God to be all in all—one cannot comprehend these by reason; it must be by a principle of faith. Let our knowledge be raised by grace to the highest level possible, and we can still never come to know the causes of such things as these are. The ground of our faith is merely divine revelation.

Now to receive a thing upon divine revelation is different from receiving it in a way of knowledge. The

Saints Can Expect Greater Glory

Scripture is clear in this, and for it take these three texts. The first is 1 Corinthians 2:9: "But as it is written, eye hath not seen, nor ear heard, neither hath entered into the heart of man the things which God hath prepared for them that love Him." Eye has not seen, ear has not heard, neither has it entered into the heart of man, no, not into the hearts of the saints by any way of knowledge, "but God hath revealed them to us by His Spirit" by revelation.

There is a great deal of difference between having things by way of knowledge and revelation. When I have things in a way of knowledge, I come to understand them upon such principles as are written in man's nature, or when I know that the whole is greater than any part I do not say that I believe it, but I know it. However, that which I come to believe is that which we have no evidence of by way of reason, but only by way of revelation. There may be many reasons given in a way of helping and strengthening us to believe the Scripture and many things in religion, but that which is the ground and bottom of all must be a revelation by the Holy Spirit, for reason can never reach those things that are the very principles of faith; they are beyond reason, such things as the eye has not seen, nor the ear heard, neither have entered into the heart of man.

The second text is 2 Corinthians 4:18: "While we look not at the things which are seen, but at the things which are not seen." They are not seen by us, neither by sense, nor any kind of reason, though ever so elevated by grace. They are not seen, but believed.

The third text is 1 John 3:2, where the apostle says, "Beloved, we are now the sons of God," we are sanctified by the Spirit of God, but "it doth not yet appear what we shall be." We cannot understand by reason, or any kind of elevation of reason, what we shall be. "But we know that when He shall appear, we shall be like Him, for then we shall see Him as He is." We do not now see God in any way of reason like we shall then, but we believe great things about God, though we are not able to behold Him. As in 1 Peter 1:8: "Whom having not seen, ye love; in whom, though now you see Him not, yet believing." You see how believing is opposed to seeing God. Therefore it is said of Moses that he saw Him who was invisible. He was invisible by way of reason, but He was seen by faith. Faith rises higher than sanctified reason. We have some kind of knowledge of some spiritual things, but this knowledge that we have must be done away. Therefore certainly there are things that we believe that are beyond our knowledge, beyond the knowledge of the saints, for the apostle in 1 Corinthians 13: 8 speaks of the knowledge of the saints and says, "Love never faileth, but whether there be prophesies, they shall fail; whether there be tongues, they shall cease; whether there be knowledge, it shall vanish away."

It's a very strange expression, "Whether there be knowledge, it shall vanish away." What, our knowledge vanish away! Shall not the saints have knowledge in heaven? Surely their knowledge, you will say, should be increased in heaven. But the text says that knowledge shall vanish away. That is, the things that we shall come to see in heaven are things that are so high and great, that are beyond coming to understand by the way of reason as now we understand things in this world. We come to have knowledge how? By the senses, the philosopher says. Thus nothing goes into the understanding but first comes into the senses. We come to have knowledge from without, and we come to work from what is presented from outside us. But this same kind of knowledge shall be done away; we shall then only be swallowed up in God Himself, in the beatific vision of the Most High; we shall see as we are seen. Certainly we are seen, that is, God knows us not in the way as we know things in this world and we shall know God as He knows us. We shall have our understandings enlightened with an immediate presence of God shining upon the understanding, and the understanding swallowed up in God Himself, so that knowledge shall be done away. So, then, there are things, it seems, in heaven that are beyond our knowledge, for when we come to enjoy those things our very knowledge shall be done away.

I remember Mr. Calvin upon this scripture saying that all the natural excellencies of men here in this world, the excellent parts and gifts they have in the knowledge of arts and science, shall be done away; and therefore those who have weak natural parts may have as clear a sight and vision of God as the most learned men in the world. Our natural abilities that we have here will not be in any way helpful to us to the knowledge of God when we come to heaven. But the poor, weak people who are of low understanding, so that they scarcely understand anything in a way of common reason, yet shall have as much knowledge of God, and as clear an insight into the nature of that pure Being of beings, and into the glorious things of God, as the greatest rabbi who ever was upon the face of the earth, for knowledge shall be done away.

There are therefore things that are beyond sense, beyond our reason that is elevated to the greatest height here in this world, and we walk by faith. This might be of great comfort to those who have weak parts here in this world; yet, though their parts are weak that will not hinder them in receiving the glorious things in heaven. But I shall leave the part about walking by sight and come to treat that which is the principal truth in the text: "For we walk by faith, and not by sight."

13

The Walk of a Saint on Earth Is the Walk of Faith

The walk of a saint on earth is the walk of faith. In handling this precious and absolutely necessary point, I shall show:

1. What the walk of faith is, and when a saint may be said to walk by faith.

2. That this is and ought to be the only walk of the saints on this side of heaven.

3. The necessity of it.

4. The excellence of it.

5. Some encouragements unto saints when they lack sight and sense.

6. Choice rules that we are to observe in the want of our sight and sense, yea, how we should exercise faith in the want of all.

7. How faith carries the soul through all kind of difficulties in this world; when sight fails, yet faith carries through.

These are the principles headings of this treatise.

1. What it is to walk by faith, briefly and more generally: A soul walks by faith when the soul walks in the way that God would have it; when sense and reason are at a standstill, what faith brings to it. Many times a Christian in his course finds all things that appear to sense and reason

to fail him, and the soul is at a loss in respect of those things. But yet faith comes and helps as a dead lift. When sense and reason do not know how to go any further, faith brings in that which carries the soul on in the way that God would have it. This is to walk by faith.

But more particularly to describe the walk of a saint by his faith:

First, the scope and end of the way of a saint is presented unto him by faith; for in a walk a man looks at some end. Now the end and scope of a Christian's walk, to what he walks, is twofold. It is either the enjoyment of communion with God or it is the glorifying of God.

OBJECTION. But, you will say, "Why is it only faith that presents this, the glorifying of God and the enjoyment of communion with Him? We may know by reason that we were made for God and we are to glorify God in our way in the course of our lives. Reason would tell us this, and that the chief good of a rational creature is in communion with God. As reason hints this to us, why do you then say that faith presents this to the soul? Though there is no faith, yet a man by reason may be convinced that he ought to glorify God, and that his happiness is in communion with Him."

ANSWER. Indeed reason will tell us these two things, but in a lower and darker way than faith does, and the happiness of man in either of these two things is but natural so far as reason carries it. Reason tells me that I am to glorify God; let me glorify God no otherwise than reason tells me, it's but in a natural way. And reason says that my happiness is in the enjoyment of God; but if I enjoy God never any otherwise than reason presents God to me, I can have but a natural happiness.

The Walk of a Saint on Earth is the Walk of Faith 143

But faith goes further in presenting this scope and end of my light. Faith tells me that I am to glorify God in the way of the covenant of grace. I am to glorify God in and by Jesus Christ His Son. In the whole course of my life I am to lift up the glory of God as it is revealed in the gospel, God in Christ. And truly, till we come to know this glory that God would have from His creatures, namely glorifying Him in His Son, in the way He has propounded Himself, we never give Him the glory that He accepts. He may so far accept it as He may bless us with some outward temporal blessings in this world, but never accepts it to eternal life.

A man who has never such strength of reason, and sees he must not live as a beast, but he must acknowledge and worship God who is the infinite Supreme Being of all things, may come to know this in the light of reason; but if he rises no higher, it is but in a natural way, and God does not accept that. But when the soul comes to know God in Jesus Christ, and comes to understand the brightness of the glory of God as it shines in the face of Christ, and so comes to honor Him in the way of the gospel, this is the scope of a Christian's walk. This is to walk by faith. And when men only look at God as the last end in a rational way, and so as the highest good, this is but merely natural. But when I look upon God in Christ as my happiness in Him, when I look upon God as communicating Himself to His creature through His Son, then I look upon the interest that my soul has in Him through Jesus Christ.

Here's the scope of my life if I am a true Christian; the work of my heart and all the actions of my life tend this way. You never knew what it was to walk by faith unless you had the scope of your life presented to you by faith, showing you what it is to glorify God in His Son and enjoy communion with God in Him. That's the first thing in the walk by faith.

2. The soul in walking by faith is guided by the rule that faith presents unto it. As it has the scope and aim that faith presents to it, so the rule that guides it is only presented to the soul by faith, and only by faith. I confess reason will go far, will present unto men many rules for the guiding them in the course of their lives. Such and such a way is suitable to right reason, and such a way is against reason; and thus far your fair, civil, worldly men go. They see what is according to the rule of right reason and so they are guided. But faith presents a better rule, the rule of the new creature. Those who walk according to this rule, as the apostle speaks of in Galatians 6:16, peace shall be on them, and the whole Israel of God. This rule is plainly the rule of the new creature, for "in Christ Jesus neither circumcision availeth any thing, nor uncircumcision, but a new creature." And, he says, "as many as walk according to this rule, peace be upon them and mercy, and upon the Israel of God." Faith shows to my soul what the rule of my way is, the rule of the new creature as it is revealed in the gospel, those gospel rules that I find in the Word that only are made known to me by revelation and faith.

Whatever revelation it is that the soul receives, it is enabled to receive it by faith. And so, if it is but merely a history, then we call it an historic faith; or if a miracle, then a miraculous faith; or if it is the revelation about the grace of God in His Son to my soul, then it comes to be justifying faith. But the nature of faith in general is that virtue or grace whereby the soul receives readily and freely the revelation of the mind of God in the gospel, where God sets out the way of bringing men to eternal life by Jesus Christ. Now faith is the receiving of these truths of God thus revealed; and those men who stick so upon it will receive nothing but what they can by reason, for they will fall short in the day of Jesus Christ. They will fall short of the rule that will guide men to eternal life. And that's the second thing, when the soul is guided by such rules as faith only presents unto it.

3. The walk of faith is when the way of the soul is likewise by faith, that is, the way of holiness is the way of faith.

QUESTION. What do you mean when you say that the way of holiness is the way that is by faith?

ANSWER. By that I mean this, that whereby the soul comes to be separated in its actions, in the course of it, from all filthiness and uncleanness; it is faith that purifies the heart; it is nothing but this. The soul walks by faith when by receiving those divine principles that are revealed in the Word it comes to be enabled to separate itself for God from all uncleanness, and to separate the actions of it from the filth and uncleanness of the world, from those mixtures that the actions of other men are mingled with. When there is that power in its believing, then a soul walks by faith. You say you believe such and such truths that are revealed in the Word, but what power has your faith to cleanse you? That's the way of faith, when it has that power in it to separate you from mixtures and base uncleanness in the workings of your heart and in the actions of your life.

4. A Christian walks by faith when faith brings strength to the soul to enable it to go on in its way. The strength that a soul gets is by faith, the closing of the soul with

Jesus Christ, and by faith drawing virtue from Jesus Christ, as the poor woman in the gospel found virtue to come from Christ. So when a Christian finds a lack of strength to the performance of any action that God requires, what does he do now? It may be some will resolve, "I will do thus and thus, and leave my sin and set upon a better course." And they go forth in the strength of their own resolutions, and perhaps they do something and reform their lives a little more than they formerly did. Yes, but this is not the walk by faith. A Christian who walks by faith, when he comes to see what God requires of him, and withal finds his own inability, goes and acts out his faith upon Jesus Christ and the covenant of grace and the promises, and there draws strength to enable him to the performance of what God requires.

5. A Christian walks by faith when faith brings in not only power to do what is required, but when there is any opposition faith enables the Christian to resist opposition, to resist whatever is in the way to hinder the walk. There may be opposition from without, persecution, when men oppose such a way and set themselves against it. Now when a Christian acting by faith can be carried on, though he is weak otherwise, yet through faith in Christ he can go through opposition and whatsoever he suffers for Christ, yet still through that which Christ has revealed to him in the gospel.

Or if the opposition is not outward, yet there may be inward oppositions, the fiery darts of the devil. You know the Scripture that says faith is a shield that quenches the fiery darts of the devil, not only that keeps them off, but quenches them. This is a strange kind of shield. A shield, especially when darts and bows and arrows were shot, would be of great use. Here the devil shoots fiery arrows. As sometimes in war they have such a device that will shoot red-hot bullets out of cannons, so the devil shoots fiery arrows. But this shield not only resists them, but quenches the fiery darts of the devil.

And so faith is an anchor in the midst of storms and tempests to keep the soul from suffering shipwreck, and not only helps against opposition, but lifts it up above discouragements and carries it through all difficulties. Now putting these three together we see what faith brings in: The soul is enabled to go through oppositions, rise above discouragements, and be carried through all difficulties. In this way a Christian may be said to walk by faith.

6. A Christian walks by faith when his great care is to go on in his duty. As for what shall become of him, that is, his success, he can commit all that to God. A Christian may be said to be walking by faith when he so orders his life that nothing troubles him in this world. What should become of him, how he should be provided for, what success he should have, his main thought is to let him be where the Lord would have him be, and do what He would have him do, and commit all his ways and successes unto God.

7. A Christian walks by faith when he can satisfy his soul by what he receives by faith as really and truly as any other men can satisfy themselves in the enjoyment of any good. Look what satisfaction to their spirits other men have in the enjoyment of what they desire; that satisfaction a Christian who walks by faith has in believing what is promised. He can find satisfaction in what is promised as other men can find in the enjoyment of what they have for the present. Oh, this is the walk of a Christian in his

way. A man who is not acquainted with this grace of faith is eager in desiring such and such things, and if he cannot have his desire satisfied he is never quiet. Nothing will calm him but the satisfaction of his desire. Yes, but now a Christian can look into the promises, and if he sees but the good thing promised he is as well satisfied in the promise as the other is in the enjoyment of his desire. Indeed, there is a great deal more satisfaction in receiving the promise than there is in what all the creatures in the world can afford for the satisfaction of their desires. If God should give us the enjoyment of all creatures in the world, they cannot so satisfy the desires of the soul as a promise can satisfy the desires of the believer. Now this is a great mystery in the walk by faith; but this is the way of a Christian, and those who understand what the walk of faith is know what I mean. Yet unto carnal hearts they seem as riddles and they think them airy conceits and notion; but such as know what it is to walk by faith know otherwise. Let but a word of promise be given out, and it's enough for a soul that walks by faith. And because this is a great point, I'll give you a text or two to show what satisfaction a promise is to a believing soul that walks by faith.

The first Scripture is in 2 Chronicles 20. Here you find that Jehoshaphat had been praying to God in the time of a great danger and, having prayed, he received an answer to his prayer in verse 17: "Ye shall not need to fight in this battle; set yourselves, stand ye still, and see the salvation of the Lord with you." Here he received the promise. Now mark verse 19: "And the Levites, of the children of the Kohathites, and the children of the Korhites, stood up to praise the Lord God of Israel with a loud voice on high." But mark this: They began praising the Lord, though they had not yet gotten the victory. Then in verse 20 we have this exhortation to believe: "Believe in the Lord your God, so shall ye be established; believe His prophets, so shall ye prosper." And verse 21: "When he had consulted with the people, he appointed singers unto the Lord, and that they should praise the beauty of holiness, as they went out before the army, and to say, 'Praise the Lord, for His mercy endureth forever.'" Was Jehoshaphat out of danger when he set singers to praise the Lord because His mercy endures forever? No, he was in as great a danger as before, only he had a promise, and having a promise he could think of nothing but praising God, for His mercy endures forever. A carnal heart would have said, "Let us first see what the success will be, and then we will sing praises." But Jehoshaphat said, "I have a promise, and I am satisfied as much in that as another man would be satisfied in the victory."

Another Scripture that is very famous for this is Psalm 108:7: "God hath spoken in His holiness." Where it says, "God has spoken," the word is, "come out." What then? "I will rejoice." He does not wait for the fulfilling of the Word. "I have the Word, and I know He is holy in all His works; therefore I will rejoice. I will divide Shechem, and mete out the valley of Succoth. Gilead is mine. Manassah is mine. Ephraim also is the strength of mine head. Judah is my law-giver. Moab is my wash-pot. Over Edom will I cast out my shoe; over Philistia will I triumph." And all this because God had spoken, for the thing was not yet done; but the prophet was as much satisfied in the Word as in the thing being done. This is to walk by faith, when the soul can be satisfied in a promise as much as others are in the enjoyment of what they have.

8. A Christian walks by faith when the soul can depend upon God alone for all, in the want of all means; when all means shall fail, and if it would consult with the flesh and blood, with means, with second causes, it sees itself as undone. But in the failing of all these means, yet the soul can depend upon God and yet conclude, "It shall be." You know that was the commendation of Abraham when his body was even dead, yet contrary to hope he could believe. Let become of means what will, yet it is God who has promised, and I can depend upon God in the want of means.

9. The progress that the soul makes in the ways of godliness is by faith. The walk of the saints is from faith to faith, from one degree to another; according as faith increases, so there is progress made in the ways of godliness; when a soul does not stand still, and is not the same as he was seven years ago, but has gotten higher and higher and nearer to God, and all by faith. Faith moves the soul still higher and higher to God in a constant way and course. That progress that a saint makes is by faith.

10. The constancy of enduring in a Christian course is likewise by faith. As it is said of Moses, "He endured," as seeing Him who is invisible, who was invisible to sense or reason. But by faith he endured. Whatever hindrances he had in his way, yet he kept on his way to the end and so received the end of his faith, even the salvation of his soul.

11. There is one more. A Christian walks by faith when he in his whole course walks as is becoming one who believes such glorious things as he does, when he holds forth in his life the glory and beauty of those things that he professes he believes. Christians profess their beliefs in very great things. They believe in God and Christ and the spe-

cial interest that their souls have in God. They believe in the covenant of grace; they believe in the kingdom of heaven, and of their everlasting enjoyment of God there. These are great things, and a man may be said to walk by faith when in his life and conversation there is a suitableness and an agreement to all these great things that he professes to believe. You Christians, when you speak of such things that you say you believe, even such things that the angels desire to pry into, do you hold forth this in your lives? This is the walk of faith, when the walk of your lives is suitable to what you profess to believe. Oh, then, put all these together and then may a Christian be said to walk by faith:

When the scope of his life and the end of it is presented by faith;

When the rule of his life is by faith;

When the way of his life, the separation from uncleanness and filthiness is by faith;

When the strength that he has to walk is by faith;

When the power to resist opposition, to be raised above discouragements and to go through difficulties are by faith;

When he can take care for nothing but only to be where God would have him and do what God requires of him, and leaves all to God;

When he can be satisfied in the promise as well as others can be in the enjoyment;

When in the want of all means, yet he can depend upon God;

When his progress and going on is through faith, from faith to faith;

When his constancy and enduring to the end is by faith;

And when in his whole conversation he holds forth the glory of his faith and lives suitable to those great and glorious things that he professes to believe. Here is one who walks by faith in his course. Here, indeed, is the life of a saint on the earth. The Scripture says, "The just shall live by faith." The Holy Spirit seems to take a great delight in the phrase, for it's very often repeated in Scripture. Thus the just lives and walks by faith. That's the first thing.

14

The Saints In All Ages Have Walked by Faith

I might show you the examples of the saints at all times, and how they have made their walk a walk of faith:
1. Enoch's walking with God was by faith is apparent in Hebrews 11: "he pleased God." And if you read the epistle of Jude, there you shall see the walk of Enoch with God: "And Enoch also, the seventh from Adam prophesised of these things saying 'Behold, the Lord cometh with ten thousands of his saints.' " Enoch, who was the seventh from Adam, believed in the coming of the Lord with ten thousands of His saints, though he it was almost six thousand years ago. Enoch's faith reached to it. Enoch, when he saw ungodly men and heard them speak hard speeches against the ways of God, looked beyond all their prosperity. It may be that he reckoned that, though they may prosper in this world and speak hard speeches. Oh, the hard speeches that many ungodly men belch out against the ways of God, yet Enoch could look beyond all their prosperity and by his faith was able to see the coming of Jesus Christ, when He shall come with ten thousands of His saints in all His glory at the great day. And the sight of this made Enoch walk on in his way. It's as if he should say, "Let others do what they will, and please themselves in their ungodly way, and walk according to the flesh, I dare

not walk as they walk. And why not? Oh, I believe in the coming of the Lord in all His glory."

Enoch, who lived almost six thousand years ago, yet by faith could behold the coming of Christ, and by that work of his faith was he kept on in his walking with God. Let men do as they please, yet he would keep on constantly in his way. And this text shows what it was that kept him on in his way.

2. Noah walked with God in his generation, and surely it was by faith too. Hebrews 11 shows plainly that it was faith: "By faith Noah, being warned of God of things not seen." Mark it, he did not walk by sight, but being warned by God of things not seen as yet, "moved with fear, prepared an ark for the saving of his house." All was by faith, and indeed that which he did could not be by any other principle but by faith.

First, he was godly in his generation, for you read in Genesis 6 that the whole world had corrupted their way. "And God saw that the wickedness of man was great in the earth, and that the very imagination and thoughts of his heart was only evil continually." This was the corruption of the times wherein Noah lived. But what kept Noah upright all this time, when men's wickedness was so great that God resolved to destroy men from off the face of the earth? Surely it was faith, for it is said of Noah that he "found grace in the eyes of the Lord, and Noah was a just man, and perfect in his generation, and Noah walked with God." What could it be but a principle of faith that would make Noah fall upon building an ark one hundred and twenty years before God would bring judgement on the earth? God told Noah that there would be a flood coming upon the earth, and therefore bade him build an ark. An ark! We never read of any such vessel to swim in the water; and Noah might have had a thousand reasons not to build such a vessel. He could have reasoned: "I am upon dry land, and should I go and build a vessel that must carry me in the water, and I alone build it? Am I wiser than all besides? They will come and mock me, and say, 'What new kind of fine thing is this that you are building?' To what purpose should I go to build an ark? I am no mariner, and I do not know how to manage it. Yes, but I must build it." And by faith he went on in his way.

And then he might have reasoned thus: "Suppose that a flood *does* come and destroy the whole earth. Is it a likely thing that the water should come upon the top of high hills?" Yet Noah believed what God had said.

And then he might have thought: "All my neighbors who are about me may kill me if they please, and put me out of the ark and take it themselves." Sense and reason would tell him so; and yet Noah went on in his way.

"Well, but suppose God puts me into the ark and keeps other men from taking it from me, but that I should have the benefit of it. Yes, but then God told me that there must be in it all manner of creatures, two and two to come into the ark, all venomous creatures and wild and savage creatures. They may destroy me!" Yes, but Noah believed that God would preserve him.

Again, "I must have an ark in which may be all sorts of creatures, and food for all these, what vessel would be able to hold this?" Yet Noah believed God. Then, "When they are there, surely the very filth that would come from those creatures would poison me!" Yet Noah still believed God.

"And when I am in the ark, and all the world shall be covered over with water, what shall become of me at last?" Yet Noah believed that God would provide for him.

God put Noah's faith to it, and by faith he went into the ark and was preserved there. It was the walk of faith that was Noah's walk in his generation.

3. I might likewise show you the walk of the saints in other times. I will speak of Abraham, how when he first came from his father's house, what a walk he took to walk into Canaan, and then afterwards into Egypt. He went up and down from place to place, having no possession at all but that of a burying place; he was in the midst of dangers and oppositions from time to time, as God tried him in the main things that He promised him. Oh, the walk of Abraham by faith was very famous.

4. There is the walk of Jacob's faith.

5. I might speak of all the patriarchs. The history of the Bible will reveal to you the walk of all their faith.

6. There is the walk of David's faith. After the promise of the kingdom, yet how he was hunted up and down in the wilderness like a partridge.

7. When Jonah was put into the whale's belly, yet still he cried to the Lord, and therein acted out his faith.

8. And we might speak of the Church of God in general, besides particular saints. Lamentations 3:24–25 shows the notable work of faith in the Church of God, when they were in the greatest distress and under the captivity of their enemies: "The Lord is my portion, saith my soul, therefore will I hope in Him. The Lord is good to them that wait for Him, to the soul that seeketh Him."

"The Lord is my portion, saith my soul." It's as if the Church should say, "If I should consult what reason says, what sense says, what temptation says, and what the world says, they would all say that God has forsaken me, that God has left me. But I will not regard what sense, reason, and temptation say, for the Lord is my portion, says my soul. I will conclude this in the greatest distress that I am in, yet still the Lord is my portion, says my soul." Still she holds to this in the midst of all her distresses, and we need not instance further particulars, for Hebrews 11 is a commentary upon my text. There you have the walk of the saints one after another, from Enoch's time to the Macabees.

And yet take this one note: They did not have the means of faith as we have; they did not have the object of faith revealed to them so gloriously as we have. Oh, when we read chapter 11 of the Epistle to the Hebrews, it should make us ashamed for and troubled in the consideration of our unbelief. Oh, the glorious work of faith that was in those precious saints.

The work of precious faith in them appeared very gloriously; therefore it should occasion such a meditation as this: "Oh! Should they who lived in the time of the Old Testament or before the New, should they walk by faith? Oh, how much more then should we who live in the time of the New Testament! Had they had but the four evangelists to read over, of Christ's coming in the flesh and the manner of His coming, being born and living, and the sermons of Christ, had they but them to have read over, and the stories of His apostles in the Acts; and the great mysteries of grace that are revealed in the epistles that we have—oh, what faith do you think would there have been in them then!"

Read but the Old Testament and see how little have you there of Jesus Christ, of the covenant of grace, and of the things eternal life. No, the apostle says that glory and immortality were brought to light by His gospel. It was little known in the time of the Law, and yet the glimmerings that they had of those objects of faith strengthened them and carried them through difficulties and oppositions whereby they were enabled to walk by faith. And so it is recorded of them for their honor, even to the end of the world. They received a good report by their walking by faith, to be an example to us. Oh, that we who are Christians and profess our belief in such glorious things as we do, we should be ashamed that we are lead so much by sense and reason as we are. Oh, let us labour above all things to manifest the glory of faith, for 'tis this that God especially aims at. It is the great design that God has to lead His people along in such a way as may magnify this grace of faith. And therefore, those of you most honor God in the world who most walk by faith. It is not those men and women who have most comforts who most honour God; it is not those men and women who have most honors in the world and most encouragements in the ways of obedience, these are not they who bring most honor to God—but those who most walk by faith.

When the Lord looks down from heaven and sees a poor creature who lacks sense, and does not have those encouragements that others have, and, it may be, you are not used in such excellent service that others are and you think thus: "Oh, the Lord has little use of me. I am not employed in such things as others are employed in. I do little service for God in my generation." Yes, but do you exercise faith in your afflicted condition, in your low condition, in that condition of yours where you seem as though God did but little regard you? Can you believe and exercise faith in such a condition? Know that this is acceptable before the Lord, and you, by the exercise of faith in your low condition, may bring more honor to God than many who have excellent parts and gifts and are employed in glorious service for God. But of that we shall have occasion to speak more of when we come to that heading of showing the excellence of walking by faith.

15

The Necessity of Walking by Faith

In a saint's walking with God, his walk by faith has a principle share. I have shown what it was to walk by faith, and then that it was the walk of the saints. This part is finished. I shall proceed unto the necessity of this walking by faith and the excellence of it. If a Christian does not walk by faith, he will certainly miscarry in his way.

First, I will show the absolute necessity that there is of it. If we will profess ourselves to be real saints and walk with God, we must have a great use of the grace of faith in all our ways. I shall show this under eleven headings:

1. The necessity of walking by faith is this, because the ways of God have a great deal of outward means in them that appear to be vile to sense and to natural reason; even the great things of the gospel are foolishness to a carnal heart. I remember Tacitus, who was a great scholar, speaking of the ways of the Jews (who were the only people of God). He said that the way and customs that God taught them was absurd and a sordid way, and yet no people upon earth had the mind of God revealed to them but them in their time. And Josephus tells of one, speaking of the Jews, who said, "They are hateful to men, and more foolish than the very barbarians. These thoughts of the ways of God have carnal hearts behind them; they are very mean and vile, and therefore there is need of faith to show us the way that we should walk in.

The Necessity of Walking by Faith 161

2. There is a necessity of faith that there may be an agreement between us and God. "Can two walk together and not be agreed?" How can there be an agreement between God and our souls but by faith? Romans 5:1: "Being justified by faith we have peace with God." Our peace with God does not come from any obedience to the commandments, but by faith. It is not the reforming of your life, though that must be, for it's a sign you are not at peace with God if you do not reform your life. But all these do not make up your peace; that which makes up your peace with God is your faith in Christ. Yes, and when a believer has made peace with God, yet afterwards he may do that which shall break his peace, at least the sense and comfort of it, yea, and so far break it as there may be a fatherly displeasure against him. Now it must be faith that makes it up. It's not enough to think thus: "I have done that which has broken my peace with God, the comfort of it to my soul, so I will amend and reform." That's good, but that's not the thing that you must rest on. "Aye, but I will renew my faith, and exercise that upon Christ, and so make the breach." Reforming will follow upon it, but the main thing that makes the agreement is the work of faith, and therefore faith is absolutely necessary.

3. Faith is of absolute necessity to walk by because many things that are to be the rule of our lives depend merely upon the will of God as it is revealed in the Word without any reason given for it. I confess there are many things of the mind of God that we may see a reason for; yea, there are some principles in man's nature that are not wholly done away with by the fall that will show to him that such and such things are rules for him to walk by. But there are others that are merely by the will of God without

reason at all, and therefore there is a necessity of faith for the discovering of them unto us.

4. There is the necessity of faith that we might come to see the authority of the rule by which God would have us to walk. Though we may by reason see something, yet there is a divine lustre and authority in the rule that we cannot come to know but by believing. In Psalm 119:66 David says, "Teach me good judgement and knowledge, for I have believed Thy commandments." Here you see that the commandments of God are an object of faith as well as the promises, which many do not think of. They think their faith is only to act upon the promises; but faith is also to act upon the commandments. That which is received by believing is received in another way than that which is received by reason. It's as if he should say, "I see some reason in your commandments, yes, but there is a divine authority and lustre and glory in your commandments that is beyond that which is to be revealed by reason, and that I receive by faith. By faith I have come to see and apply that infinite mercy and glory and authority that there is in Thy commandments." Oh, that we could but learn to believe the commandments as well as to understand them, or to be convinced by reason of them that we are not to lie, nor swear, nor profane the Sabbath, nor commit adultery, nor do any act of injustice. These things we may convince men's consciences of, yet they do not believe the commandments, that is, the infinite dreadful authority that is in them, for this reason does not bring with it power to the soul. Oh, those in whom God works faith come to see and to apply another kind of authority in the rule than they have done heretofore. Therefore,

there is a necessity of faith in our walking, even to make the commands of God to come with power to our hearts.

5. There is a necessity of faith that we might come to see the reality of spiritual things. They are all but notions to us until we come to have the use of the grace of faith in the course of our lives. We may talk of justification, of sanctification, of adoption, of reconciliation, of the love of God spread abroad, of the Spirit of God, of being guided by God's Spirit, of the privileges of the saints, and such things, but they are mere fancies and notions to us till we come to have faith. According to Hebrews faith gives real being: "Faith is the substance of things hoped for." It gives substance to them and makes them to appear as the most real things in the world. Therefore, there is a necessity of faith for making spiritual things to be realities to the soul.

6. There is a necessity of faith in our walking that we may be able to see through the colors and vain shows and pretences that are upon the ways of sin. We shall be guided and deceived otherwise by color and pretences and fair shows that are put upon these, those gildings that are upon the ways of sin. Sin will appear very fair and specious; the most dangerous and desperate ways of sin will present themselves seemingly desirable to us unless we have a piercing eye of faith to look beyond present things. Faith is necessary in our walk that we may see through those paintings and coverings that are put on the ways of sin, that we may look beyond things that are present. It is said of carnal hearts that they do not see afar off. "If these thing be in you, and abound, they make you that you shall neither be barren, nor unfruitful in the knowledge of our Lord Jesus Christ; but he that lacketh these things is blind and cannot see afar off" (2 Peter 1:8). He can see only

things that are present; but you who have the knowledge of Christ can see afar off. Oh, there is a great necessity of faith in the course of our lives.

7. There is a great necessity of faith in our walk in the course of our lives, because God seems in His way to go often so contrary to what He speaks in His Word. I have showed you that sense and reason are not enough, and now I am to show you the necessity of faith because God in His ways will appear to go so contrary to His Word that we shall not be able to see them. I have shown you that God in His works sometimes seems to go contrary to His Word, as in the case of Abraham.

I'll give you some other examples, such as God's bringing His people Israel to the land of Canaan. He promised to them land that would flow with milk and honey, but at first they were brought into the southern part of the land which was, for the greater part, the most barren; only some little might be fruitful. But it was of all the land the driest part and most fruitless, and this is the reason for that expression that we have in Psalm 126:4, where the psalmist says, "Turn again our captivity, O Lord, as the streams in the south." The streams that were in the south were mighty refreshing and comfortable; there were streams in other parts of the land as well as there, but they were most comfortable because the southern part of the land was so dry and barren, and therefore any streams in the south were very refreshing unto the people. And thence is this phrase: "Turn again our captivity as the streams the south." It seemed to be contrary to what God said of the land, that it would flow with milk and honey. But God brings His people into the barest place at first, and the reason for it was to try their faith.

The Necessity of Walking by Faith

Likewise you read in Judges 20:28–31 that God made a promise of victory to the people, and yet you shall find that although He promised them victory, at first there was a slaughter made, and such a slaughter as encouraged the enemy to hope for a victory over them the second time. After God makes the largest and fullest promises of mercy to His people it's His usual way to seem to go quite contrary. Oh, the ways of God are unsearchable, and His judgements are past finding out. If there is not faith, we shall presently be offended when we see that the works of God seem to go contrary to that Word that we have thought we have believed in.

8. There is a necessity too in respect of the strong oppositions that the saints meet with in their way. They meet with the devil, the world, and the flesh, and all opposing them in their way. The oppositions from the world come by ways of scorn, contempt, and persecution. And it may be there is opposition from their kindred, from their parents, from their governors, from their nearest yoke-fellow, bosom friend; if there is not faith to help against all these the soul would never endure. Moses endured by seeing Him who is invisible.

There are inward oppositions that come from temptations within, from strong corruptions that are within the soul, and unless faith comes in the soul will soon fade away. It is a notable Scripture we have in Isaiah 64. Mark there the complaint of the Church in the time of their affliction and trouble: "We all (says the prophet in the name of the Church) do fade as a leaf; and our iniquities, like the wind have taken us away" (verse 6). Oh, their hearts were down and discouraged, but what was the reason for this? "And there is none that calleth upon Thy name, that stirreth up himself to take hold on Thee" (verse 7). This was the reason why they faded away like a leaf.

When a leaf lacks moisture and has the sun to dry it, it soon fades away. So it was with them; they met with trouble and opposition, inwards and outwards, and like a leaf they faded away. But it was upon this ground, because none stirred himself up to take hold of God because they did not act their faith upon Him. In the time of their sufferings, when they were in a low and afflicted condition, when temptations and troubles came, then they should have stirred themselves up to have taken hold on God. Had they but had the use and exercise of faith then, they would not have had cause to have made such complaints. There is therefore a necessity of faith for overcoming strong oppositions.

Set reason or experience many times against oppositions that a Christian meets with in his way, and these are but paper walls to keep bullets off. But now faith can set even Christ Himself and the promises of the covenant of grace, and these are as a brazen wall against oppositions. It is faith that quenches the fiery darts of the devil. A man has strong temptations, and there comes in the fiery darts of the devil thick upon him. Now he begins to reason with himself: "Here are these temptations, and why should I yield to them? If I yield, I shall bring shame to myself. Alas, this is but as a paper wall in comparison; and if I yield to such temptations, I shall bring a great deal of trouble and affliction to myself and my conscience will not let me alone, but fly in my face."

These are some things to help against temptations, but they are all as paper walls in comparison to the actings of faith upon God and Jesus Christ. If the soul could but stir

The Necessity of Walking by Faith

itself up to take hold upon God and Jesus Christ, this would strengthen it far more and be as a brazen wall in comparison of the other.

9. Another thing that shows the necessity of faith, and a special thing to be considered, is this: We must walk by faith, all our walk, or else it will be to little purpose, because it is by faith that we come to please God, and without that it's impossible to please Him. "Without faith it is impossible to please Him" (Hebrews 11:6). Whatever you may do in the way of God, yet if there is not the exercise of faith in it, it is not accepted. You think you walk with God in this duty and the other; you pray continually, you hear the Word, receive the sacraments, converse with saints, and do such and such good actions. These are well to do, but unless faith comes in and mingles, none of them pleases God. It may be before you were acquainted with the ways of gospel you were very careful in your course; you kept your constant times in prayer, attended upon the Word, lived very well among your neighbors, read the Scriptures, and were careful to come to Christ's appointments. But if you were not in the walk of faith, these things were not pleasing to God. They are indeed not so displeasing as the neglect of them would be, however, and therefore they ought to be done even by unbelievers, for materially they are good. And it is better to do that which is materially good than not to do it at all.

Yes, but if you speak of pleasing God in order unto eternal life, and in the complacence that God takes in such things as He is pleased with in His saints, they do not please Him so. No, it is the work of faith in the very action that must make it acceptable. If you offer it up to God it must be by faith. Oh, how necessary is faith to make everything pleasing to God. Therefore consider this note: It's not enough that you are believers in general, that is, that you have faith in Christ, and so you have pardon of sin, but this shows there is a necessity of putting forth faith in every action.

10. Further, the happiness of a Christian, the last end that a Christian has is supernatural; therefore, as I showed when I opened what it is to walk by faith, faith brings in revelation of the end of our walk, and here it shows the necessity of it. If our end in all our actions is above reason, then we have need still of the use of faith in everything that we do so that we might always have the right end. It is this indeed that commends an action in morals; it's the end that makes the action good. And so in divinity, it's not what the action is, but what the end is; this crowns all. The necessity of faith is in this to carry on all our actions to a supernatural end, to an end beyond reason.

11. It is faith that is so necessary because the efficacy of all means that we use for any good depends upon faith. God sets us about the use of means for the attaining of such ends. God never ordained means that they should help us to attain such ends by virtue in themselves. God ordained means to convey Himself through those means, and the efficacy of them must be by using them in a believing way. Such and such means God has appointed for such ends, but if I make use of those means and think that they have any virtue or efficacy for the attaining of those ends, I frustrate the good of the means. If I would use them in a profitable way, I must mix faith with them. Yes, I use these means, but it is the love, goodness, and mercy of God I trust in the use of these means. If I use the means to preserve my natural life, I should exercise faith there.

The Necessity of Walking by Faith

Asa is blamed for using the means of the physician, and trusting in him and not the Lord; but then much more when I use means for my soul. I come to the Word and prayer and the other ordinances; there's no efficacy at all in all these any further than faith is mixed. You know what the apostle says, "The Word did not profit them because it was not mixed with faith." And so in prayer; the prayer of faith will save the sick, but if you trust and rely upon your prayers you will spoil all. The thing indeed must be done, but that will not do it; and you will find your prayers will come to little. And that is the very reason why the times of prayer in your closets and in public have come to so little. You have prayed against such and such corruptions, but when a temptation has come you have been overcome as before and you wonder at it and think, "Lord, what shall become of me? I have prayed against this sin I know not how many times, and thought that Thou hadt come in sweetly to my soul at such a time. I had such enlargements, and I went out in the strength of my prayer and thought that verily I should be able to overcome my sin, but I find I am as weak as ever." It's because you trusted in the means. It's true, God appoints such and such means, but did you believe in your prayer and act your faith on Christ, the promise, and the covenant of grace in prayer? Oh, it is faith that is necessary in the use of all means to make one to have profit and benefit in them, and therefore certainly Christians must look to that especially to walk by their faith.

And thus you see the necessity of it.

16

The Excellence of Faith

The walk that is by faith has a great excellence in it many times.

1. It has a great excellence because a saint who walks by faith has higher apprehensions of God and the work of God than others have. The apprehensions that others have of God are very low and mean in comparison to the one who walks by faith. One who walks by faith can see God upon His high throne. Others see only the back parts of God, but the one who walks by faith beholds His glory with open face. When Moses would see the glory of God (Exodus 33, the latter part), God said that He could see His back parts; but the gospel says that with open face we behold His glory. We not only see the footsteps of God, but we see Him in His face, see Him in His glory and excellence upon His high throne, and that's a most excellent thing.

2. That soul that walks by faith carries on all actions in a high and supernatural way, and makes his very civil and natural actions to become heavenly and supernatural; it makes noble every work and puts a price upon everything that a man does. I remember Luther had an expression concerning poor milkmaids who are believers and walk in their callings in obedience to God, and as a fruit of their faith they have more glorious actions when they go up and down with their milk pails than all the victories and tri-

umphs of Alexander the Great, Julius Caesar, and all who live upon the earth. Why? Because they walk by faith!

And that Scripture in Hebrews 11 concerning Joseph is very famous concerning this. What was the act that Joseph did? He carried the bones of his father into the land of promise. When his father Jacob died he would be buried in the land of promise, and Joseph carried the bones of his father there, and that makes it an act of faith. A very low and mean action, one would think, to go and bury his father's bones in such a ground, yet it's made a glorious action and recorded by the Holy Spirit as a most excellent action. Why? Because it was the action of faith!

So the meanest work of your callings, if it is but done by faith, is excellent and honorable before the Lord. Now you who are in very low callings, servants who are but cleaning the house and doing the meanest works, yet still if it is as a fruit and effect of your faith, and your acting faith in the action, you make it a supernatural and a glorious action that God highly esteems. Many poor people who are employed in mean things are discouraged; they think that others who are employed in the great affairs of state and churches are the happy people, but your faith will make your lowest and meanest actions more glorious than theirs.

3. The excellence of walking by faith is this: Faith brings in whatever good there is in Christ, in the covenant of grace, and in the promises, and makes it sweet unto the soul. Now for one to walk up and down in the whole course of his life, and not only to suck in the sweetness that there is to be had from these when first converted, but every day to be sucking in the sweetness of the promises, and so enjoy whatever is in Christ and the covenant

of grace, it must be an excellent and a glorious life—and this is the life and the walk of faith. Oh, it is a most delightful walk then, the walk by faith; and so far as we exercise faith, so far we bring delights into our souls. If there is any delight and good to be had, either in Christ, in the covenants, and in the promises, it is enjoyed when we walk by faith. Surely then we need not walk droopingly and heavily and sadly, if we had but hearts to exercise faith.

4. Those who walk by faith converse much with God. As they have higher apprehensions of God than others, so they converse much with God, for faith is that which takes off the heart from the creature and presently carries it to God through the creature. When one who has faith in continual use has to do with any creature, he has communion with the creature, but instantly his heart is upon God in it. And in the use of an ordinance, presently his heart is upon God. It does not stay in any thing, but flies to God and rests itself in Him and converses with Him. And when he awakes in the morning, presently faith is acted, and there he converses with God in heavenly thoughts and meditation. And when he comes to prayer he converses with God; when he walks up and down in the world and sees the sun, moon and stars, he converses with God in them. So too, when he has communion with the saints, he converses still with God. All who walk by faith converse much with God, and therefore it is excellent.

5. Faith is the grace that in a more eminent way honors God, which I have many times spoken of, especially once handling the preciousness of the grace of faith. It honors God above all other graces because it attributes nothing to the creature, but all to God. And it glorifies that in God that God Himself most glories in, such as the

The Excellence of Faith

mercies of God and the faithfulness of God. In His mercy and faithfulness God is glorified in a more special manner, for His mercy is over all His works and faith gives glory to that in a most eminent manner. It gives God the glory of His power too, and of His wisdom, and of all His other attributes. Abraham believed and gave glory to God. Likewise, the men and women who walk by faith glorify God. You think if your hearts were more holy than they are, and more heavenly-minded than you are, you would glorify God. It's true, that would help you, but if you could believe more than you do you would glorify God more, and the other things would follow by themselves.

6. It is an excellent walk, the walk of faith, because by it the soul is freed exceedingly from fears, from doubts, and from misgiving thoughts in the course of it. Where faith is not strengthened a Christian walks as one in the dark is afraid of every bush. So long as a saint is but little acquainted with this mystery of godliness in walking by faith, fears are there every day. If there are but any stirrings of corruption in his heart, then God is an enemy presently, and I am a reprobate and a castaway. Such conclusions are ready to be where there is not the use of faith. And if God seems but to absent Himself a little while, it seems that He is gone forever and never will come again. And if the heart finds temptations to come in strong, the soul says to himself, "One day I shall perish by the hand of this Saul." Oh, the fears and doubts and misgiving thoughts and jealousies that there are in the hearts of the saints in their walk while they do not walk by faith; how they are bewildered in their course. When the soul walks by faith, it is helped against all these fears, doubts, and misgiving thoughts that some souls (if they had it) would give a

world to be free from. "Oh," says some poor soul, "if I could be but freed from these, what a happy life I could lead." If you could learn but to exercise your faith in the course of your life, these would be dispelled even as the mist passes away before the sun, and temptations would little prevail with you. As I hinted before of faith, it would quench the fiery darts of the devil. Temptations would not prevail so as they did if the soul could but act out faith more.

7. You shall do great things for God in walking by faith. You think your grace is small and you shall never do much for God, but faith helps to do great things for God, though the saints' graces are but weak for the present. Those men who have the greatest measure of sanctification do not always do the greatest things for God; but such men as can act out faith most and have the greatest measure of that are those who do the greatest things for God here in the world. They are His best instruments.

8. Besides, you will make great progress in the ways of God. You will go on quickly. Those who walk any other way walk very slowly; they walk as a sick man with his staff in his hand; he can go on but slowly. But such as can walk by faith would have no need of the staff of experience, or the staff of comfort, and of reason and such things. Such a one can walk on quickly in God's ways, yea, run, if need be. A man who walks in any other walk, if he meets with any stumbling blocks, he does not know how to get over them; but one who walks by faith, walks on high above stumbling blocks. If a man walks in the midst of stumbling blocks he cannot walk fast, but if he can get above them, he speeds his way more.

9. What shall I speak more about the excellence of this? It's that which causes uprightness in the heart. "I am God all-sufficient, walk before me and be upright." This is as much as to say; "Abraham, act your faith upon Me as the All-sufficient God in all your ways; do not look upon the creature, but upon Me, and then walk before me and be upright." What's the reason for the unevenness of the saints walking in their way? It's for the want of faith. They do not walk by faith, and therefore, if they meet with this and the other difficulty, they will turn aside out of the way. But where the soul can walk by faith, it walks in an upright line to God and has no impediments about him one way or the other.

10. By walking by faith we come to have the present enjoyment of the end of our faith. "Receiving the end of our faith, even the salvation of our souls." It is not only you *shall have* the end of your faith, but you have it; *Receiving* the end of your faith. The saints have heaven now in their hearts; every step they take they enjoy the end of it. That is the great excellence of it, to enjoy the end and reward of all our actions. In keeping God's commandments there is great reward. While I am in action I have heaven. I enjoy God and heaven and my last end. I have the blessing, the happiness of my last end in every thing I do. This is to walk by faith indeed. Many walk heavily in their conversations and yet have some hopes that at length they may get to heaven; but by walking by faith we have eternal life *now*. It's a comfortable walk when a man is walking and sees the end of his journey before him; that encourages him. But this is more than seeing the end of the journey, it's the enjoying of the fruit of our journey.

11. And then the excellence of it is in this: It is so useful in all estates and conditions we have need of faith. If God puts us in prosperity, if we do not act out faith there our prosperity will spoil us and slay us; if God changes our condition into adversity, there we must have the use of faith too; if we are in sickness, or in health, faith still is needed; a single estate, married condition, whatever our condition or employment is, yet still faith is needed. The usefulness of it shows the excellence of this our walk by faith.

12. It is that which brings a good report too, a good report even by God Himself. God commends this grace above every grace: "For by it the elders obtained a good report" (Hebrews 11:2). They were spoken ill of by men, but by their faith they obtained a good report; their names were dear and precious in the eyes of God. The elders obtained, or were attested unto. Faith honors God and gives Him a testimonial (John 3:33), such as that in Deuteronomy 3:4. God therefore honors faith, according to 1 Samuel 2:30, and gives it His testimonial, as here, the elders are eternalized in this notable chapter, this little book of martyrs, as one fitly calls it. I beseech you to consider this, you who take care of your names. Oh, you cannot tell how to bear the loss of a good name, to be reviled and condemned. Here is the way to have a good report; it is by faith. And the truth is, though many will speak ill of you, yet go on in a constant way walking by faith and the Lord will clear your names. Trust God for your names and liberties and comforts and all, and you shall find your names will be cleared by God and kept by God as boxes of precious ointment. They all obtained a good report.

13. Last, this is the excellence of it: It will make one die comfortably. There is no more comfortable death to a man as this when he meets with God at the end of his walk; for when death meets with him in this walk, it can never look terrible. If you have gotten out of the walk of faith, into the walk of sense, the common course and road of the world, death will meet you and be terrible to you, even as the king of terrors. But if death meets with you here, it will look upon you with a very cheerful and amiable countenance. In Hebrews 11:13 it is said: "These all died in faith, not having received the promises." Only in passing observe this concerning the last point, and mark how the words are twice repeated: "For by it the elders obtained a good report" (verse 2), and then in verses 39–40: "And these all, having obtained a good report through faith, received not the promise, God having provided something better for us"). But the main place for our comfort in death is in my text, and that which follows upon it: "For we walk by faith, not by sight."

What follows then? We are confident and willing rather to be absent from the body and to be present with the Lord. In walking by faith and not by sight we are confident and willing to be absent from the body; let death come when it will, it shall be welcome; it cannot come amiss because we walk by faith and not by sight. The great reason why people are afraid of death is because they walk by sight so much. Walking by faith will make the soul to be willing to be absent from the body and to let the soul go freely out. When a vessel has no vent, the liquor will not run out; but give it vent and then it will run out. So here, when the soul is not willing to go out of the body, let it have but a sight of those heavenly things that faith is able to let in to it and the soul will presently be willing to be absent from the body.

Thus then you can see the excellence of the saints walking by faith.

17

An Exhortation to Strengthen Faith

Let us improve this a little to stir up saints to strengthen faith above all. I find that many souls are very careful to strengthen other graces and make great complaints of the want of them; but they are not so careful of this, neither do they make such complaints of the want of this. Few are so much troubled for the want of this as for the want of humility and meekness and heavenly-mindedness. You shall have many complaints thus: "Oh, that I could get my heart more humble and more broken, then I would be happy. But, oh, I have a hard heart." But get your heart more believing than it is and you will be as happy. And so another complains, "Oh, if I could overcome my passion, get mastery over myself and be meek in my carriage. . . ." But if you could get more faith, that would be better and would help against your passion. "Oh, if I could overcome my evil thoughts and pray better, how happy I would be." Say rather, "Oh, that I could believe more and exercise faith more. Oh, that I could get influence from Jesus Christ more." And this would make you happy. If you do not walk by faith you will lose your way quickly; you will lose sight of the end of your faith and that will discourage you, and then you will lose your very way itself, and you will be mightily ensnared and be ready to be drawn out of your way and stumble therein, if you do not exercise faith. But by faith you will keep in sight the end of your way, and keep your way, and be delivered from stumbling blocks, from snares in your way.

Now to the end that you might strengthen your faith, remember to practice this choice rule: When you cannot put forth your faith in a particular promise, yet hold to the main covenant, to the great and the grand promise. And when you cannot put forth faith in a conditional promise, yet put it forth in an absolute promise. Sometimes I cannot see particular promises that I can act upon, but what's the covenant of grace promise? Look upon the infinite freeness and the fullness of the covenant of grace then.

OBJECTION. But it may be some will say, "I do not know whether it belongs to me or not."

ANSWER. Consider this, there is fullness of grace and freeness of grace in the covenant, and therefore say "Why may it not belong to me? I am not excluded, therefore let me keep that before my soul in all my distresses." The sure keeping and presenting of it before the soul is a special means to draw forth the virtue of faith.

And then, though I do not see a conditional promise, I cannot apply that. For example, when God says, "Blessed are those that mourn, for they shall be comforted, and blessed are the poor in spirit," oh, I do not mourn, nor am I poor in spirit. I do not find the condition of those promises in me. Yet there are other promises that are absolute and carry the condition of those promises in them, such as, "I will take away the heart of stone." He does not say, "I will take away the stony heart if you do thus and thus," but it is an absolute promise to all who can cast themselves upon it and it requires no preceding conditions. This is a mighty help in our walk by faith.

First, by faith look to the grand promise and the covenant in general when you cannot apply particular promises.

An Exhortation to Strengthen Faith

Second, though I cannot apply a conditional promise, yet let me look unto an absolute promise and let my soul hang there. That will be enough to support me for the present and let me exercise faith there. But more of this, and the helps of faith, I shall come to treat under the next heading, that is, what the soul should do when there is want of sense, when God absents Himself and the soul has lost the sense of God and His love and mercy. And when God's works do not seem to go with him, but rather against him, how the soul should help and relieve itself in that condition; for here indeed is the only act of faith when sense fails. Oh, that is the soul that walks by faith, that knows how to make use of it when all the props of sense fails—but more of that in the following discourse.

The life of a saint on earth is a mystery, for it is to walk by faith; and it is no marvel that the men of the world do not understand the way of the saints. They wonder at what they mean in denying themselves so much as they do, and doing things that they can see no reason for. Hence it appears then that it must be a mystery to the world because it is a walk by faith. Galatians 2:20 is a very remarkable place for this. There the apostle says, "I am crucified with Christ." As for all the honors and preferments in the world they mean nothing to me, I am crucified to all things. Those who lived with him might stand and wonder: "What's the matter? Why should Paul be crucified to all the preferments he might have had?" He was a man of great esteem and credit, yet he was crucified to all things. But though I am crucified, yet I have a life; though I am crucified with Christ, yet I live. I have a life beyond all the things in the world. What is that? "Yet not I, but Christ liveth in me; and the life which I now live in the flesh, I live by the faith of the Son of God." I am crucified and am willing to be dead to all the things in the world because I have another life, the life of the Son of God, which I have by faith. Oh, the way of godliness is a great mystery that the world does not know. The world looks upon them as a company of dead creatures; but they have a principle by which they live that is beyond the thoughts of men. But this I shall pass from and proceed.

Suppose you cannot, for the present, have use either of conditional promises or absolute promises, yet there is some help. The soul is to endeavor to cast itself upon God's attributes, that is, to work after God that way and do what it can to close with God's name. I confess we can never have any assurance of God's love and His mercy until we have it in the way of the covenant. But it is one means to help the soul seek after God when it is out of the sight of a promise, to venture itself upon the attributes of God, such as upon the mercy of God, for He is infinitely merciful in Himself, and the power of God and the goodness of God. I confess these things can never fully satisfy the soul unless it knows God in Christ, yet they may be some help to keep the soul from departing from God. It's true, the attributes of God in themselves can never be a sufficient object for saving faith, yet they may be some stay of the heart for the present to keep it from departing from God, and in such a way wherein it may come to find God so much the sooner.

That was the support of the poor woman of Canaan who we read of in Matthew 15. The poor woman there had no promise to rest upon, neither conditional nor absolute; for when she came to Christ she cried, saying, " 'Have mercy on me, O Lord, Thou son of David; my daughter is grievously vexed with a devil.' But He answered her not a word. And His disciples came and besought him saying, 'Send her away.' But He answered and said, "I am not sent but unto the lost sheep of the house of Israel. What have I to do with you? I am not come to you.' And then He told her, The children's bread must not be given to the dogs.' " Christ staved her off from all kinds of promises.

But she cried out, "Lord, help me." She looked upon Him as a Lord, as one who had infinite power. She could not stand reasoning that the promise belonged to her; it's as if she should say, "Though I acknowledge I cannot tell how to rest upon any promise, yet Thou art good and merciful. Lord, help me." It would be more comfortable if we could pitch upon a particular promise and anchor there, or upon the covenant in general, or upon a conditional promise. But if we are barred from all that we have, neither conditional, nor particular, nor absolute, yet still there is something to help us in looking upon God in His attributes, though not sufficient to make it to be the object of a saving faith.

18

Help For the Soul In Walking by Faith

But further, to proceed in helping the soul in its walking by faith, there are these four things that I intend to prosecute in this point:

First, to lay before you some principles of faith that faith may help itself upon.

Second, to give some encouragements to a soul that wants all sense; when God is quite out of sight, yet what encouragements the soul may have.

Third, I shall lay down some arguments to move your hearts to put forth acts of faith even in the want of sense when all is out of sight.

Fourth, I shall give some rules of direction that the soul should do in that great case of the want of sense.

These are the four headings, and I shall not be large in any of them.

First, I shall lay down eight conclusions or principles that may be for the support of faith when sense and reason is at a stand.

PRINCIPLE 1. Whatever my case is, yet I have to deal with God, with the infinite and glorious God, who has the compass of all things before Him, who does not only look upon things that are now present, but with one view He sees all the whole frame and latitude of all things. Our knowledge is like a man going up to the top of a tower and looking through a little cranny; he sees those things

Help For the Soul In Walking by Faith 185

that are right before him; he does not see the things that are on this side or that, only those things that are right before the cranny. But the knowledge of God is like a man's knowledge who is on the top of the tower, and if there is an army of men in the field, with one view he can see them all. Now the soul, when it is in any difficulties, should look thus upon God: "I have to deal with that God who has the compass, the latitude, and the issues of all things before Him." And upon this you can see how faith helps itself. "Yes, though I cannot see how such and such a thing can be, yet I have to deal with an infinite God who sees all before Him, and He may see ways and means that I cannot see. And although I think that such a thing tends to such and such an evil, yet God, who looks down beyond the present, may see a great deal of good coming a long time after by those things that seems to be hurtful for the present."

The great reason why men do not believe, and when sense and reason is at a stop and their hearts sink, is because they look no higher than themselves; they do not look at God who has the compass of all things in His view. If they did, this would quiet them. A child, when he is at a stop and does not know what to do, will commit himself unto his father and thinks, "My father knows." So should we do when we are at a standstill: We should consider that we have to deal with a God who has the latitudes and issues of all things in His eyes at one view.

PRINCIPLE 2. God's Word is more to be stuck to than His works. We are more to rely upon a word than upon a work of God. That is a principle that would be a mighty help to faith. Let's search and see whether we have a word to warrant us in our way, whether any word from God holds forth any comfort to us.

OBJECTION. You will say, "When I read the Word, I have some comfort. Oh, but when I see how things are working, then I am quite taken off."

ANSWER. Lay up this as an everlasting principle: God's Word is more to be rested upon than the works of God, for God puts His Word as an object of our faith, but God never makes any single work of His to be an object of our faith. We have had occasion already to show you how that God's works many times seem to be quite contrary to His Word. Take one single work without reference unto another work and it would be quite contrary to His Word. I remember I instanced the case of Abraham, when God promised him to make his seed as the stars of heaven and yet he must kill his son. The work that God would have him do was quite contrary to His Word. Then too God bid him go from his own country into the land of Canaan that flowed with milk and honey; yet the first thing that he met with was a famine in the land of Canaan. Oh, therefore, rest on the Word of God rather than on any works of His, for we cannot, nor would God have us understand His works many times. God loves to be in the dark in His works, but His Word is light; the Scripture says that God's ways are in the dark, but His Word is always called light, therefore that's to be rested upon.

PRINCIPLE 3. All good that is in all creatures in the world is eminently in God Himself, in the very being of God, so that the soul enjoys all good there is in all creatures. I beseech you to observe it, when the soul enjoys God, it not only enjoys a good that is better than all creatures—for everyone will say that the mercy of God and the goodness of God are higher and better than all the good that there is in all creatures—but we must understand it yet further than that. Not only that the enjoyment of God is better than having all creatures, we must also understand that whatever good all creatures in the world have for doing good, all that power and sweetness and comfort that is scattered up and down in several creatures, is all united in God. Thus, while I have the Lord, I have all power in all creatures; and that's a mighty principle of faith.

For now I lack sight; it may be I see this and the other creature working against me, and I see the lack of help in one and the lack of help in the other. But if I can have a real sight of God, to see all the good that is in all creatures to be in Him, this is a wonderful support. Then if I have to do with nothing but God Himself, I have enough, for I have all there in Him. It's as though a man does not have such and such herbs that grow in a garden; perhaps he has neither rosemary, nor thyme, nor sweet-marjoram, yet if he has the water that is stilled out of these herbs, he has the virtue and quintessence that is in every one of them. So the soul that has union with God, and has their portion in the Almighty, has the quintessence and virtue and efficacy of all creatures in God Himself. That's the third great principle in the helping of faith in the want of sight and sense, in any case of trouble that the soul is in.

PRINCIPLE 4. All creatures that we look upon, those that may afford us any help, all their power depends upon God. They have neither power to do good or hurt any further than God gives out His power and concurs with them. No creature in heaven or earth has the least power to do the least hurt any further than God is pleased to let Himself out through those creatures. He has the absolute command of all. These things are granted in general, and you are ready to say, "Who does not understand them?" It's true, it's an easy matter to convince men of that, but if it comes to examination, the very ground of the shaking of our faith when we met with any trouble arises from the want of the use of these principles. Let these be laid to the heart; let there be a right and a sound understanding of these and it will be a mighty help to our faith.

PRINCIPLE 5. <u>The way of God in working for His creatures is often a way beyond all means whatsoever. God delights in working (and especially for His servants) beyond all means of all creatures and contrary to all means, above all means, without means, and contrary unto means.</u> This is the way of God in His working for His saints. I confess the way that God uses to work for others (for the men of the world) is but the way of a general providence. It is a very useful consideration, this one note, to consider the difference of the working of God towards the generality of the men of the world and the working of God in reference to His saints. The working of God towards the men of the world is the working of His general providence and no further. They can expect no more; and if God works any further towards them, to bring good to them or to help them, God has a special aim somewhat beyond them.

<u>But as for His working towards His saints, there the right hand of God is stretched out, the right hand of God's power, and it is glorious in excellence.</u> That is, God, <u>in working for the good of His saints, takes a great deal of delight in going beyond all means, without means, and contrary unto means.</u> And indeed, those actions of God

that He minds His saints in more especially are such. Hence are all those expressions that you have of the right hand of God and the excellence of His power. "The excellence of His power is over Jacob." It's true, it's the power of God that works all good to all creatures in the world, and God causes His general providence to be working for good to them; but His excellence is over Jacob, that is, to work beyond, without, and contrary unto means. There's the glory of God. God says, when He works for His people, "Such kind of works as are ordinary for Me to do when I am working for others will not serve to manifest My love and respect to My saints. No, I'll go beyond and without and contrary to them."

Oh, that this might have a double use upon our hearts, not only to strengthen our faith, so that when means are wanting and come short and seem to go contrary, we will walk by faith. Oh, but let us likewise learn from hence to be more than ordinary in our service for God. He is more than ordinary in His working towards us. Let the soul lay this up and take this as for granted, that God in His special working for His people and churches works otherwise than He does for others. He works beyond and without and contrary unto means; and He commonly puts the sentence of death upon a thing before He gives it.

PRINCIPLE 6. God, in His dealings towards His people, seldom does any great matters for them but He puts the sentence of death first upon it before it's done. He does not usually come to help till just before they are ready to die, until all seems to be gone; then their extremity is His opportunity. God would not give Abraham a child till Sarah's womb was dead, and he was, as it were, dead. So if you examine the ways of God towards His people, He usually brings them into the shadow of death, and there is a sentence of death, and then appears the grace and mercy of God towards His people. And so the apostle speaks of God's dealing towards him in 2 Corinthians 1:8-9: "We were pressed out of measure, above strength, insomuch that we despaired even of life." Yes "we had the SENTENCE OF DEATH in ourselves." But to what end? To the end "that we should not trust in ourselves, but in God which raiseth the dead."

Hope is never elevated higher than when our state in the eyes of all men is at its lowest. You must not therefore, when you find your condition brought so low as to say, "This is beyond all my strength, and God does not tempt His people beyond their strength and therefore surely God is gone, help is gone." No, now is the time for God to come, if ever, when the sentence of death is put upon a people. Oh, how often have you found God sometimes coming in when you have given up all at sea, and if the wind had not turned just at that instant you would have been gone. But then has been the time for God to come and work for your deliverance, when the sentence of death has been upon you, because God would have all the glory of it to Himself. And that is the sixth principle.

PRINCIPLE 7. Whatever promise we have in all the Book of God, to any particular of the people of God, that promise may every godly man apply unto himself, being in the same condition that he was in. If you read in the Book of God how He has dealt with any of His saints when they have been in any extremity or difficulty, God has given out promises to them to assist them, that is a warrant for you to lay hold upon that promise as if it were made to you in particular; and this is a great help to faith. These two

Scriptures are generally known: The promise that God made to Joshua when He said, "I will never leave thee, nor forsake thee" (Deuteronomy 31:6), and that which the apostle, in Hebrews, applies it to all Christians who lived in those times (Hebrews 13:5). They might have said this promise was made to Joshua and not to us, yet the way the apostle applies the promise is a general rule for us, that whenever we find any promise in Scripture concerning any particular godly man, we have a warrant to make use of it just as much as if God had called to us from heaven by name and said, "Thomas, or Richard, I will do this and this for you." That is the seventh principle.

PRINCIPLE 8. There is no condition that any of the people of God can be in, no condition so dark and so wanting comfort, as is a sufficient plea for unbelief. Though your condition is never so dark and dismal in your own eyes, yet, remember, it can never be so dark, so dismal, so void of comfort, of helps, as should give you any ground for your unbelief. I'll give you one Scripture that may serve instead of all for this. Isaiah 50:10: "Who is among you that feareth the LORD, that obeyeth his servant, that walketh in darkness, and hath no light? Let him trust in the name of the LORD, and stay upon his God." Who is there that walks in darkness and has no light? No light at all, nothing but darkness, dismal darkness; you walk in darkness because your walk is not the walk of faith. But who is it that walks in darkness and sees no light of comfort at all? What should he do? Let him trust in the name of the Lord and stay upon His God.

This is for whoever is among you that fears the Lord; it's those indeed who fear God, so they must be qualified, and their desires are to obey the voice of His servant.

Mark it, the Holy Spirit speaks of two things that godly people in their greatest weakness may find:

First, the fear of God is upon their hearts. Indeed although they cannot do as other saints, they cannot overcome their corruptions, yet the fear of God is upon them.

Second, they obey the voice of His servants. They can appeal to God, who knows all things, that there is nothing their souls more desire than to be obedient to God, speaking by His servants to their souls. And though it's true they have no power to do the things that are required, yet there is the obedience of the heart. Well, then, who is it? Whoever it is, though never so weak, though never such stirrings of corruption in them, yet if they thus fear God and their hearts lie under the authority of His Word, so as to be willing to yield obedience to the voice of God by His servants, though he walks in darkness and sees no light, he sees no comfort, no way of succour for him, yet let him trust in the name of the Lord and stay upon his God.

Thus there is no condition so dark and dismal to any who desire to fear the Lord and walk in His ways but they may exercise their faith in trusting in the name of the Lord and stay upon their God. And thus you have these principles laid down for to ground your faith upon which you should lay next to your hearts, for you may have use of every one of these in your walk.

19

Encouragements to the Soul In Walking by Faith

As for encouragements to the soul in its walking by faith, consider these particulars:

1. God offers Himself unto those to whom the gospel comes, so as He is willing to deal with them in the way of a covenant of grace and not a covenant of works. This is a special help and encouragement to the soul that is in darkness and sees no light, and has no sense of the patience, love, and mercy of God; yet, O soul, look up to God. "Oh, the sight of God," such a soul will say, "is terrible to me. The Lord is a consuming fire, and who can stand before the everlasting burnings? Oh, who can endure the consuming fire?" But, O soul, look up again and behold the Lord offering Himself to deal with you in the way of the covenant of grace.

OBJECTION. Yes, but I do not know whether I am under the covenant of grace.

ANSWER. Yet when your ears hear the glad tidings of the gospel, know that it is nothing else but God coming to offer Himself to your soul in the way of the covenant of grace. Had we to deal with God in the way of a covenant of works—cursed is every soul that abides not in everything that is written in the book of the law to do it—then every thought of God might be terrible to us. I verily believe that this is the main ground that holds many under a spirit of bondage and causes them to walk in a disconsolate and distressed condition, and not walk to by faith, because they look upon God as having to deal with Him in the way of a covenant of works. They see God to be a holy, just and righteous God, and see His law as righteous. Now they are conscious to themselves of having broken His law, and their consciences being defiled with evil works, and having guiltiness upon them, they are not able to put forth any acts of faith to believe in Him.

But on the other side, could this soul come to behold God offering Himself to it, to deal with it in the way of a covenant of grace, and the Lord speaking thus, for so He does, "Oh, you wretched sinful soul who are cast and undone by the covenant of works that first was made with mankind, you are undone and by that must perish forever. But behold, there is a second covenant, a covenant of grace, wherein I am willing to deal with the children of men, and through that covenant that I have made, that is, believe and live, I am He who justifies the ungodly. And in that covenant there is a way of satisfaction for the sons of men; there is acceptance even of the desires and endeavors of the souls of poor creatures who are otherwise full of sin. Yes, there is acceptance of their souls through the covenant of grace, and that to eternal life. It is through that covenant that I am willing to have to do with the children of men, with you in particular to whom My gospel comes to be preached; not too deal with you merely as I am the Creator of all things and you a creature, as I am holy and you are sinful, but willing to deal with you through My Son and to apply the purchase that My Son has made." Oh, if we could but come to see the Lord so, in the midst of all fears and troubles we might come to exercise our faith and walk by faith rather than by sense, beholding God in this manner. Indeed, without beholding God thus we shall never be able to take a step of faith in our walk. And that's the first encouragement.

2. All the good that God does for His creatures, especially in order to eternal life, is for His own name's sake. It is out of grace and nothing else. It is because mercy pleases Him (Micah 7:18). It's not because you can please Him, for He will have mercy on whom He will have mercy and whom He will He hardens; it is merely because He delights in mercy. It is from arguments that are in His own bowels and not from arguments that are or can be in you or any creature. What an encouragement is here for the soul to exercise faith, a soul that walks in darkness and can see no light. I can see nothing in my own heart but a dungeon of dismal darkness. Oh, but I hear that the fountain of all God's goodness unto His creatures, of all the good that He does for His creatures in order to eternal life, is merely out of free grace and because mercy pleases Him. Then why may there not be a way for me to exercise faith, though my condition is never so sad in itself? That is the second encouragement.

3. There are no qualifications in the creature that are required by God as a condition of our believing. God does not say that if you are thus and thus, then you have the right to believe, and so you come to have a right to Christ: there is nothing before faith that gives a right unto faith. Indeed, there may be something before that may take away some hindrances and stops, and so may help us towards believing, but nothing before faith that can give us a right to believe. Therefore, for men to say, "How do I know that I have a right to believe?" we answer, if you can

believe your believing gives you a right to believe. It is my believing that makes me to have an interest in the riches and in the grace of the covenant to apply it to myself, but there is nothing that can give me a right to believe. If the gospel is preached and I find the Lord working upon my heart to draw me to believe, if the gospel is preached, the Lord gives me the liberty to it, that is, not that I may think that I have my part in Christ. All to whom the gospel is preached have right to this: If they can find that in their hearts to cast and roll their souls upon the infinite, free, full, and rich grace of God in the gospel, they may do it. They need not stand to plead whether it is not too much boldness in them so to do, for you are invited to do it freely. Come and drink of the waters of life freely; and you who have no money, no worthiness at all in you, yet the way is made over to you as well as to others. And that is a third encouragement.

And if at the first time, when we come to believe, there are no qualifications required to give us interest to believe, then surely at all other times we are not to reason that because I am thus and thus, therefore I may *not* believe. Let your condition be as bad as it can be afterwards, yet surely it is not worse than it was at the first; you are not worse off than before, or at least it cannot be so ill but that this rule may encourage you.

Yes, though they have sinned against knowledge and after profession of religion, yet still this holds a truth that there are no precedent qualifications that give you a right to believe. It does but that which may make way and take away hindrances, and therefore you may still be encouraged in the want of all sight and sense yet still to exercise your faith.

4. The great glory and design that God has in the world is to glorify Himself in the way of His free grace and faithfulness towards the children of men. God delights in the glory of His power, in the glory of His wisdom, in the glory of His bounty, and in the glory of His justice; but the great masterpiece above all things is the glory of His grace, in the glory of the riches of His grace, mercy, and faithfulness. It is this that the Lord delights more in than He does in making the world. God has made one world, and He could make a thousand worlds more by one word of His power. If God pleased He could make a thousand worlds more by one word, yet God does not so much delight in making worlds as in showing forth the riches of His grace to the poor, wretched creatures who have undone themselves. This is the great masterpiece of God by which He will be honored in to all eternity, when the soul shall think, "If that mercy may do me good that shall be so great as God shall have the chief glory of above all His works, and that God takes more delight in above all His attributes, if that mercy will do me good, then this is offered to me in the Word, and therefore I may have encouragement to believe."

5. As it is God's great design to magnify His grace above all His works, so it's as delightful to Christ to enjoy the end of His death as it can be to any of you to have your souls saved. Christ takes as much pleasure in, and accounts it as great a good to Him, to have the end of His death as any of you can account it to have your soul's eternally saved. You think thus: "Oh, such and such a mercy that I have need of, what a benefit would it be to me if God would grant me this mercy. Oh, if God would save my soul, pardon my sin, and bring me to eternal life,

how happy I would be." What, is your heart set upon such a mercy and do you so prize the pardon of your sin and the saving of your soul? You cannot prize it more than Christ prizes the fruit of His death; you cannot get more good by your salvation than Christ shall get by having the purchase that He purchased by His death.

You know that Scripture in Isaiah 53:11: "He shall see of the travail of His soul, and shall be satisfied; by His knowledge shall my righteous servant justify many." This is the travail of Christ's soul: He is satisfied. If you could see the salvation of your soul, and God should, as it were, in a map show you all the glory that you should have in heaven to all eternity, would not this satisfy you? Now when Christ sees the travail of His soul, that is, in bringing life and salvation to sinners, this is as great a satisfaction to the heart of Christ as your salvation can be to your own soul. The consideration of this may be useful to help you to believe in the want of all sense whatsoever.

6. God withdraws Himself from His people and brings them into such a condition wherein they are without all kind of sense of His love, and there is nothing but darkness. The Lord has many good ends why He does this. He does that which is very sad to the hearts of His people, but it is not so evil, for God many times has excellent ends for which He does it. He takes His servants off from the props of the creature, and from the props of sense and reason, to the end that He may be all in all to them. If there was no other end why God withdrew Himself from His creatures but that He might show to them what their condition would be like forever if He eternally forsook them, if God never had any other end, then you may be much discouraged in the want of sense.

But consider what an encouragement is here for you to think thus: "Indeed, my condition is sad, if God has no other ends but to forsake His creature. But have not I heard out of the Word many times that God has very gracious ends, and that He not only aims at His own glory, but at the good of His creature in withdrawing Himself, and much good has come by it? It has been a means to withdraw the hearts of His servants from the creature and to unite them more strongly to Himself. Then why should not I make the best interpretations of God's dealings as may be? Before I was afraid that surely God had utterly forsaken me; but then I heard that He has many gracious ends why, for the present, He withdraws Himself from the hearts of His people, not only many good ends why He outwardly afflicts His people that many are convinced of." Oh, but that God should intend good in withdrawing Himself from their souls, that they cannot see so much. But you, afflicted soul, that is tossed with tempests and with temptations and troubles, know that God has many times gracious ends even in withdrawing Himself from the very souls of His servants.

God withdrew Himself from the very soul of Christ for a time, for so He cried out: "My God, my God, why hast Thou forsaken me?" Therefore do not think that it is always in hatred, and that it will be a certain forerunner of God's separation from you. Certainly God loved His own Son dearly when He cried out so; and indeed that may be a mighty help to our faith, when we consider not only what God does many times to His dear saints, but to His own Son. Consider also that God did not withdraw Himself from Christ only for satisfaction (for so it was), and to show that we had deserved that the Lord should eternally withdraw Himself from us, but it was that He might be a merciful High Priest to us. "We have not an high priest which cannot be touched with the feelings of our infirmities, but was in all points tempted like as we are" (Hebrews 4:15). In all points? Why? You are tempted with poverty, so was Christ; you are tempted with disgrace, so was Christ. "Yes, but I am tempted with inward and spiritual afflictions, with God withdrawing the sense of His love, mercy, and goodness—what should I do there?" Christ was tempted so too "in all things," the Scripture says. And why was He tempted? It was that He might be made sensible of our infirmities, that He might be a compassionate High Priest to us. Therefore mark the exhortation that follows upon it in verse 16: "Let us therefore come boldly unto the throne of grace, that we may obtain mercy and find grace to help in time of need."

So I shall conclude for the present with that exhortation. Do you lack sight and sense? Oh, walk by faith, and let this be an encouragement and help to you for the exercising of your faith: We have such a High Priest who was touched with the feelings of our infirmities. Among other particulars you may see it in that cry: "My God, My God, why hast Thou forsaken Me?" I make no question but it was one special end why we have this very suffering of Christ in His soul recorded in Scripture, and it was when He was afflicted outwardly, yet He was inwardly afflicted at the same time. Christ was apprehended as a malefactor and so accused. He was imprisoned and forsaken by His friends. He was in the hands of wicked men, yea, in the hands of wicked men so as to be put to death by them, and there made a gazing stock to all the world, and scorned at in the midst of His afflictions. We do not usually scorn at men when they suffer, even though they suffer for their sins; but Christ was scorned at. Now if ever there was a time for God to shine upon Him and to give Him the sense of His love, one would think it should be now. Oh, but now at this time God withdraws Himself from Him so far that He cries out in agony and bitterness of soul, "My God, My God, why hast Thou forsaken Me?"

You are to make a twofold use of this:

First, here is a satisfaction to God's justice. Christ, by being forsaken for a time, has delivered all believers from being forsaken by God eternally.

And it is likewise a use of very great importance that believers should make of it. Christ is set out as a pattern before us, and we are to arm ourselves with the same mind.

He is set forth unto us as a High Priest to show unto us that He was put under such temptations as these are. It was to the end that He might pity us and have compassion on us in our temptations and trials. It was to the end that our faith might be helped. If we would ever be brought to such a condition, to be without sense, so as to look upon God in the greatest of our afflictions to have forsaken us, yet then cast up an eye to Jesus Christ and behold Him thus forsaken, and know that as here is satisfaction to justify for you, so here you have an example of God's dealing with His own Son whom His soul loved; for certainly the soul of God always loved Him. "I know Father, Thou always hearest Me," and so He always loved Him.

Certainly the Lord had gracious ends in forsaking Him, and this is set out as a pattern to you for the helping of your faith when all sense is wanting. And had we nothing in all the Book of God to help us to exercise faith in the want of sense but this example of Christ, and the dealings of God the Father with Him, it would be sufficient to help us to walk by faith when we have no sight nor sense.

The walk of a saint is the walk of faith; there's nothing that manifests us to be saints but this, walking by faith and not by sense.

I shall add one further encouragement that may help very much, especially to a soul who is humbled before God and is panting after the grace of God.

7. Consider, when you are afraid that God should cast you off because you have no sense of His love, what would God get by it if He did cast you off? If you can but bring it to this, that God shall get as much by receiving you and saving you as He shall have by casting you off, why should you not have encouragement to believe and exercise faith in the want of sense? When you have the most dismal thoughts of all, and sense is furthest off, what do you think God will get if He should cast you off?

OBJECTION. You will say, "He shall have the glory of His will. He shall show forth the absoluteness of His will in it. And why should I look any further into what reasons God may have?"

ANSWER. To that I answer, first, if God may have the glory of His will and yet save you too, yea, and have the glory of His will rather more in saving such a soul who is making after Him than He should have in casting him off; and surely if God may have a great deal more glory—then you may have a great deal of encouragement to believe.

For if He has the glory of His will, it is but His will *upon* you; but in saving you He may have the glory of His will *of* you, and that's more glory. You shall passively glorify His will, that is, you shall be a subject, as God may make it to appear before men and angels that He may do what He pleases with you. But when you shall come and be subject to His will and lie down at His feet, He has the glory of His will actively upon you, and this is more.

Again, God shall have the glory of His power by casting you off, aye, but when you come and fall down before Him and tremble at His presence, He has it more.

Yes, and He has the glory of His power in showing mercy as well as in destruction. We have a notable Scripture for this in Numbers 14:17–18. Moses is pleading for the people and says, "I beseech Thee, let the power of my LORD be great, according as Thou hast spoken, saying, 'The LORD is longsuffering, and of great mercy, forgiving iniquity and transgression.' " "Let the power of my Lord be great," so that it seems the power of God appears in forgiving iniquity and transgression as much as in destruction. If God should destroy you, indeed a glorious power of His would appear in your ruin; but there will appear as glorious a power of His in forgiving you as in destroying you. And may not this be a great encouragement to exercise faith in the want of sense.

OBJECTION. Yes, but God is a just God and delights in the glory of His justice; and He will have the glory of His justice, it may be, upon me.

ANSWER. Nay, but you may be encouraged to believe this: He may have as much glory of His justice in saving you as in destroying you. Yes, and He may have it more in saving you than in destroying you.

First, you tremble before God's justice. If there was no more that that for the heart from a free act, not from a forced act, but freely, even that is as great a glory of God's justice as God has from all the damned in hell. In destroying the creature God has no more glory of His justice than when the creature shall, by a free work and not by a forced work, come in and tremble before God's justice and subject itself to the justice of God, and acknowledge God's righteousness and justice if the Lord should destroy it. The glory that He has upon the damned is but punitive, and that is not so much; but the glory of His justice He has in you, in that you freely come and acknowledge it, and tremble before it, He has it actively, and this is more.

Second, there is a way for God to have the glory of His justice and yet to save you.

OBJECTION. You will say, "Though I come freely to acknowledge God's justice, yet God's justice is not glorified fully."

ANSWER. Yes, but there is a way wherein God may save you and yet have the glory of His justice fully, and that is in Jesus Christ. Now what a transcendent encouragement is this to believe when there is nothing that can be conceived wherein God shall have glory one way, but He may have it the other way, and have it more abundantly. If God destroys the creature, to what end is it but that He might have glory. Now if God may have His glory and save the creature, may not that creature have hope and ground to believe, when the Lord has provided such a way of salvation as His glory shall be no loser at all? And especially this when the soul considers that God has begun already such a work upon it, wherein He is in a way of glorifying Himself in the soul as much as if He should have destroyed it. And thus much for the encouragement of believing in the want of sense.

I am willing to be somewhat large upon this point because it is so needful. Though I may treat things that are but as riddles to many, yet to those souls who lack the sense of God's love these things will not be too large, but their hearts will greedily embrace them. But because the want of believing in the want of sense is easier to speak of than to do (for it is one of the hardest things that are to believe in the want of sense). Therefore I will further proceed in the way of motives to labor to draw the heart to the work of believing.

20

Motives to Draw the Heart to Believe in the Want of Sense

The great hindrance of believing in the want of sense is that the heart thinks that the work of believing and the work of humility will hardly stand together. It thinks that it is not fitting for me to believe, but to be humbled before God. Yes, it is fitting for others; they may believe, but I am a wretched, vile creature and the work that I have to do is to be humbled.

MOTIVE 1. Therefore the first motive is that there is as great humility and obedience to God in believing as in any other way, and so this will take away the two great hindrances to believing. The first is for me to be humbled. The second is that I am very sinful, and it is for me to look rather to walk in obedience to God and to do what God requires before I should believe in the grace of God.

Now humility and obedience are as eminent in believing as in any way whatever in which it can be made eminent. If a creature would study wherein to show the greatest humility and obedience, it must be in believing in the want of sense, for there is much self-denial in it. The heart of man is set upon this; it would gladly have something in itself, but faith is an emptying grace; for it is to deny its own thoughts, and to venture itself against its own sense. Here is a great deal of humility, for men to do things when they see no reason and encouragement for it.

Though a servant is neither very humble nor obedient, yet he will do some works if he has present encouragement before his eyes and sees present reason for it. But here's the trial of an obedient servant: If he is required to do that which he sees no encouragement for before his eyes, nor able to understand the reason of such things. Though it's true, it's his master's will that he should do it, yet he rather apprehends there will come a great deal of trouble upon it rather than good. Yet if he does it at the command of his master, he shows himself to be humble and obedient in this.

So certainly humility and obedience is shown as much in this grace as in any: It is the most humble and most obedient Christian who is the most believing Christian. This is the command of God, that you believe in His Son. The command of God above all other commands is that you should believe in His Son. And when the Holy Spirit expresses the subjection of the heart to God, He expresses it in the subjection of it to the gospel in the way of believing in Christ, whether there is sense or not. Romans 10:3: "For they being ignorant of God's righteousness, and going about to establish their own righteousness, have not submitted themselves unto the righteousness of God." This is a great submission for the heart, for the heart to rest upon a righteousness that is above itself, a righteousness that is in Christ, and when it sees no righteousness in itself, yet to submit to the righteousness of Christ.

"I have many times thought that if I were thus and thus, God would show mercy to me, but the Lord has withdrawn Himself, for I am a wretched, vile creature." But the gospel presents the righteousness of Christ, and you must submit all your thoughts to the righteousness of Christ.

Christ. Here is the submission of your hearts: Those who are humble before God, for the want of sense, think with themselves that they are willing to submit to God. If you should ask them, "Would not you gladly bring your hearts to be willing to submit to God?" they would answer, "Oh, yes, oh, that I could do it." Well, if you would submit to Him in anything, submit to the righteousness of Christ; submit all your thoughts and all the reasonings of your minds that are against the righteousness of Christ, submit them to the righteousness of Christ. Here is humility, here is obedience, for the soul to give up itself to the workmanship of God. It's true, I have nothing in myself, but I give up myself to the workmanship of God and Christ, to do with me what He pleases. Here is evangelical obedience.

MOTIVE 2. It's the safest way in the want of sense to exercise faith. What will you do, poor soul, who has no sense of the love of God in Christ? You will be glad to take the safest way; and certainly this is the safest way, for if you think when you want sense to be striving and laboring in the performance of duty till sense comes and then you will believe, indeed, you do not take the safest way. But if you can cast yourself upon free grace as it's tendered in the gospel, this is safer than any other way, for you shall see the danger of the other.

There is a great deal of danger in putting yourself under a covenant of works; if you go the other way, it is as Paul said concerning circumcision: "If ye be circumcised, Christ profits nothing." Why circumcised? Because that was an eminent work of the Law that was required of them, and, indeed, a seal of the whole Law. Though it was a seal too of the gospel, and of the righteousness of faith, yet it was an eminent work of the Law besides that those who were circumcised bound themselves to the Law in it and therefore Christ did not profit them. So if you think to get joy and the comforts of the Holy Spirit in any other way but believing, you are in danger of putting yourselves out of the covenant of grace and into a covenant of works.

And besides, there is much danger in it this way because by seeking to get it by working and laboring in the performance of duties you are in danger of never having it, for it's never likely to come that way, but by our believing. You may be working any other way all your lifetime and never come to have it. Or if you should come to have it that way and so think to ground your faith upon your sense still, it will be most dangerous. If you should have some joy and encouragement by your striving, and then ground your faith upon that, you are likely to miscarry in your faith, and that faith likely to come to nothing in conclusion. It's a dangerous thing to ground faith upon sense. Yet many of us seek to have our faith be the fruit of our joy rather than to have our joy be the fruit of our faith. We should rather lay the foundation of faith and then the joy that comes after; that's the right way. If after an act of believing you come to have joy, that joy is right; but if after an act of joy and work of sense you then think you can believe, you may suspect that faith not to be right. Indeed, good works are a nurse to faith, but good works are never to be the mother of faith.

But further, it is safe in this because it will free you from the danger of temptations. If you are striving and struggling in duties to get the sense of God's love, if that is the thing and not by the exercise of faith, you will be liable to many temptations. For example, you will be striving and struggling, but will not get strength, and then comes the temptation to think: "I have labored and striven and nothing comes of it, and therefore surely God does not love me."

Yet there will be this temptation: "Would it not be as good for me to break off and leave off all? I see that nothing comes of my duties." And so you will have a temptation to turn aside after vanity; you will be weary of the performance of duty within a while, though now you set upon it. Therefore it is the safest way for the exercising of faith at the first in the want of sense to look upon the grace of God in Christ as it is offered, and to cast the soul upon it.

OBJECTION. But you will say, "Though there may be danger in my standing upon sense, yet I should exercise faith presently; there is danger of presuming, and therefore by avoiding one evil I would run upon another."

ANSWER. To help you against this I will show you what presumption is.

First, presumption is to trust in God's mercy outside of Christ. That's the first thing in presumption, and most men in the world who presume do so upon this ground, because they hope in God's mercy. But they do not apprehend the mystery of the gospel, how God's mercy is to be let out unto them through Christ, and that there is not one drop of God's mercy but is to be communicated through Christ and in no other way. Yet most men rely upon God's mercy and hope that God who made them will save them, and so they trust upon God's mercy outside of Christ. Whatever hopes of God's mercy you have outside of Christ is presumption, for no creature has anything to do with mercy but in and through Christ.

But perhaps those who live under the gospel will say no, they will not trust in God but through Christ.

The second thing, then, is trusting that God will save them through Christ, and yet they mistake Christ and do not understand Christ aright. For example, they trust in God's mercy through Christ only to save them from danger, to save them from the punishment of their sin, merely for such self-ends as they may be delivered from punishment. They see no excellence in Christ but as He is one who could deliver them from punishment; this is presumption too. But faith is when the soul is not only convinced of this, but sees by the Holy Spirit that all the mercy of God is to be conveyed through Jesus Christ.

But further, the Lord shows to the soul the excellence of Christ not only as one to deliver it from punishment, but as one in whom there is all good to make the soul happy forever. There is grace in Christ as well as pardon, sanctification as well as redemption and glorification. There is the bringing in of the soul to God, union with God, and the enjoyment of God in Christ; and that's the happiness that my soul desires, not only to be delivered from hell, but that I who was broken off from God through sin may now come and have union with Him, and so be happy in the enjoyment of God as my portion forever—and thus I trust upon God's grace in Christ. Certainly this is not presumption. <u>Though you could do this at such a time that you cannot find any ability in yourselves to perform any duty, yet if you do now cast yourselves upon the grace of God in Christ that you might have life in Him—not only that you might have pardon and to be delivered from hell, but that you might have life, do this as soon as you will—this is not presumption.</u>

A third thing wherein presumption consists is this, for men to believe that Christ is theirs, and that they shall have believed upon false grounds. For example when men shall believe that Christ is theirs and God will have mercy upon them and save them. Why? Because they are not as bad as others; because they do some good things, live honestly among men, and serve God as they speak; because God blesses them in their outward estates; because they have prayed to God and He has heard them, and such things. Thus they believe that mercy is theirs and they shall be saved, and because good people think well of them and they keep company with them who are godly. Here is presumption.

Therefore, when I exhort to believe in the absence of sense, I do not exhort to this, that you should presently conclude in your own hearts, "Well, Christ is mine and I shall certainly be saved." No, but the work that I exhort to is this: To cast your souls upon the grace of God in Christ for life and for salvation. It may be you cannot reflect upon your hearts and say, "I am sure I shall be saved," for to exhort men and women that they should persuade themselves they shall be saved is not the thing, for that must be a work of Christ's Spirit. But I am speaking of the first act of faith whereby the soul, though it does not apprehend that it shall be saved, yet will venture itself upon the grace of God in Christ. "And if I perish, I'll perish this way," says the soul. This is that which I exhort to, and not to make any conclusions that certainly you shall be saved upon such and such false grounds. No, if afterwards you come to make conclusions it must be upon the testimony of the Holy Spirit witnessing to your soul that this act of yours in casting your soul upon Christ is a true act indeed, and not a mere delusion. For that may be the way of coming to have sense, not that only, though that's one way, but by the testimony of God's Spirit witnessing to me that this work of mine in thus going out of myself and rolling my soul upon the grace of God in Christ is a true work and not a delusion.

It's true that where this witness of the Holy Spirit is, it is ever according to the Word, and there will follow gracious effects from it. Certainly there may come an assurance this way, and maybe as certain as I am in that when I see the light of the sun by the light of the sun I need have no evidence that I see the light of the sun but by the light of the sun itself. And so there may be that certainty of the soul's believing by the evidence of the work itself, by a work of enlightening by the Word; and this is another manner of ground of my joy than because I am not so bad as others, and because God blesses me in my outward estate, and the like. No, I have found such a mighty work of God upon me carrying me to His Son, and I find now such an evidence of the Spirit that this is the work of God, that I am become a new creature. I am not only not so bad as other men, but I find I live by new principles, have a new rule and new ends that I propound to myself in all my ways. But this is after this work of faith, from the effects of it, so that it is evident that your believing in the want of sense is not presumption, but the safest way that can be taken.

MOTIVE 3. This is the soonest way to get the sense of God's love.

OBJECTION. You will say, "Why, if I could find myself to be able to overcome my corruptions and perform such and such duties as others are able to do, then I am persuaded I would have the sense of God's love. But I think I shall never have it until then."

ANSWER. You go the furthest way about it. Whether ever God will give it that way or not is a question. But if God should be so indulgent as to give it to you at last, yet it will be a great while first and you will be held under the spirit of bondage a long time.

OBJECTION. You will say, "We cannot do it in ourselves."

ANSWER. It's true, any more than you can do anything else; but let there be that power that you endeavor to put forth in other things. Endeavor to put it forth here, and endeavor it in the first place (I speak to such as are sensible that they do not have the sense of God's love unto them, and are longing and thirsting after it). That, I confess, will come among the directions, but it's necessary here for the right understanding of what I mean when <u>I affirm that it's the speediest way to get sense, to labor to put forth an act of faith even presently. You complain of your dead heart, and say that if it were quicker you would then believe. Let this assure you, there is no such quickening grace as faith is.</u> "The just shall live by faith"; and the Scripture tells us that the Lord has quickened us. "You being dead in your sins, and the uncircumcision of your flesh, hath He quickened together with Him" (Colossians 2:19). How? "Having forgiven you all trespasses." So that the quickening of the heart, you see, is in the work of justification; it's in the forgiving of our trespasses. We first would have our hearts quickened, and then we would believe that our sins are forgiven; no, but believing in the grace of God for justification is the way of quickening. Sanctification follows after justification, and therefore is the soonest way to get grace. And what sense you would have in the love and goodness of God is by believing;

that's the speediest. You only beat about the bush in any other way. You would get it abundantly sooner this way in laboring to stir up acts of faith, in believing in God, than you can do in any other way whatsoever. That may be done in some heart this way that may be done in some months or years in any other way.

MOTIVE 4. <u>Labor to stir up faith and to walk by faith in the want of sense, because, even when sense fails, then is the proper time for faith to act, and then faith appears in its own native excellence, in its proper colors.</u>

As for love (by comparing one grace with another we shall come to understand either grace the better), for me to love another when I see all things lovely in them, and when there is nothing that in any way discontents me, here does not appear any great excellence in love. Who cannot but love such a one when all things lovely are there? But when you can love even though there are cross dispositions, though there are many things done that displease you and are unlovely; when your love goes through a great many difficulties and though there is much water it cannot be quenched—this is love. Water will quench a little spark, but it cannot quench a great deal of fire; yes, this love is something indeed.

So it is here in faith. It is not so much for a man to believe when he has all kinds of encouragements for his believing, when he has sense to help him too, and experience, and all things go according to what is spoken in the Word. But for me to believe though things seem to go quite contrary to my faith, though things are cross, here is the proper act of faith and the excellence of faith. <u>For me to be able to believe against discouragements, as it was the commendation of Abraham's faith to believe against hope</u>

and above hope; whatever there is against my faith yet to believe, is faith indeed. Certainly there would be no great need of the grace of faith if we had always sense, if we had always God's light, and heaven, and all the glory that God has laid up for His people; if this were always this in our eyes, then there would be no great need of faith, and therefore in heaven such kind of faith as this will fail. The Scripture says that faith and hope will cease, but love continues; it's because then they shall always have sight. But when there is no sense, then appears the proper act of faith. Therefore labor in the want of sense to put forth faith.

MOTIVE 5. Believing in the want of sense is a most glorious work itself; there's a great deal of glory in it. I remember three things that Luther spoke of that are the hardest things to be done in the world. One is, "to believe things that seem to be impossible." Another is to "trust in God and believe in Him when He shows Himself to be an enemy." And the third is to "hope in things that are deferred." These are the hardest things to believe, things that are impossible. But though they are very hard, yet certainly they are glorious works of faith. Another speech Luther had is this: "Faith, if it is strong, acknowledges God." What, though God seems to leave the soul? Yes, then a strong faith will acknowledge God to be a receiver of the soul at that time. And again he says, "When God seems to persecute a soul, yet it will acknowledge God to be the helper of the soul at that very time; when God seems to damn a soul, he acknowledges God to be a Savior at that time."

Here is the strength of faith, and this is a glorious work of faith, to acknowledge God, who forsakes, to be a re-

Motives to Draw the Heart to Believe 217

ceiver of the soul; God, who seems to persecute, to be a helper; and God, who damns, to be a Savior of the soul. Here is a glorious act of faith, and certainly it's glorious in the eyes of God and in the eyes of the blessed angels. It's such a glorious act that even the very angels do not attain to. There is no act that we read that the angels have in heaven greater than this: "though He slays me, yet will I trust Him." That act of Job was a glorious act. The Scripture does not mention any more glorious act of any of the angels in heaven than that act is. They have perfect sight, they see the face of God and have no temptations to distrust God. But in the midst of temptations, and when God seems to come out to kill a soul, yet then to rely upon His grace in Christ is a most glorious act of faith.

MOTIVE 6. As faith is most glorious in itself, so it is that which honors God more than any other grace. You know what the Scripture says of Abraham, that he gave glory to God by believing. Why, would you not gladly give glory to God in the greatest measure that you possibly can? If you would, it is by walking by faith when God is out of sight, and when all things that might otherwise be encouragements seem to be out of sight. You give God here the glory not only of His power and goodness and mercy, but His faithfulness.

It's a notable story I remember Plutarch had concerning Alexander, in reference to his physician Philip. Alexander had a physician who was named Philip in whom he trusted much for his faithfulness, whom Permenio sought to defame to Alexander, and wrote to him that he was bribed and corrupted by Darius with large promises of great riches to take away his life by giving him poison. Some time afterwards, the letter being brought to Alexander, he did not make any of his close associates acquainted with it. But that he might show the confidence he had in Philip, when the hour came that he should take his medicine Philip came into the chamber and brought the cup in his hand with the potion he should drink. Alexander then gave him the letter, then cheerfully took the cup from him, and showing no manner of fear or mistrust of any kind put it to his mouth and drank of the potion before the letter could be read. By what he did, it as if he should have said, "See how you are accused, yet for all that I am not afraid to put my confidence in your faithfulness still." I would apply it thus: Did not Alexander honor his physician very much by showing all the world how he trusted him? And though he had such a temptation to suspect him and to call him into question, yet he would hearken to no such temptation, but would venture his life upon him. If Alexander had given his physician never so much, it could not have been such an honor to him as to show how he would trust him in such a case as this.

If we hear such and such an accusation of such a one, yet if our hearts can trust in them, still it's a great honor that we put upon them. Now, then, consider what honor faith puts upon God. "It's true our lives are in God's hands," says temptation and base unbelief. "God will leave you one day. God intends no good to you. All that you have is but to prepare you for further wrath; you will perish at last in such a way as this. God will fail you at last." Temptation would persuade us that God rather hates us in all that He does than intends love to us. Yet, when temptation has said what it can, yea, when things seem to work as if God would destroy at last, faith says, "But though He kills me I will trust Him. I will venture my life upon Him;

Motives to Draw the Heart to Believe

yea, I will venture my life upon God and His ways. I am resolved whatever I suffer, and whatever I meet with in those ways here, I'll lay down my life and venture my eternal estate upon God in these ways of His. It may be that the world scorns me and mocks me, and says, 'They are but fancies and conceits,' but, says the soul, "Here I have pitched my anchor; here I'll venture my soul and eternal estate upon God."

Oh, what honor it is to God when we believe against sight. The Lord was so well pleased with this work of Abraham's faith that He renewed His covenant with an oath. He swore to him then what He would do for him. Oh, it so took the heart of God that the Lord then took a solemn oath that He would be his God and the God of his seed. Oh, when the Lord sees a soul put such an honor upon His faithfulness, then He not only promises, but swears to do good to that soul. But when men will tempt God through unbelief, the Lord swears against them, as against the people of Israel. <u>The Lord is provoked against unbelief, when you tempt Him that way. As they said, "And can God prepare a table in the wilderness? And there are the children of Anach and walls that reach to heaven." So God said, "What, are these the things that will cause you to distrust in Me and to think of turning back to Egypt? I swear in My wrath that you shall never enter into My rest."</u>

And so on the other side, when things seem to go quite contrary and yet the soul says, "Well, come what will come, let me suffer never so much, I'll venture not only my credit, liberty and comforts, I'll venture not only my present, but my eternal estate, and I'll lay myself at God's feet." Now when the Lord sees this, oh, it's that which pleases Him at the very heart, and He is ready to swear that this soul shall never miscarry. Oh, it's a grace that much honors God.

MOTIVE 7. And it is grace that argues much love for God. You say, "Oh, that I could love God more." Those who believe most love most; as I hinted before, love is seen in that I will not regard any accusations. The main work of love is this, that it makes me so that I can trust myself with my Beloved, as it is said of the good wife in Proverbs 31, that the heart of her husband can trust in her. Let any come and accuse his wife never so much, yet his heart can trust in her. Strong love cannot stand with jealousies. Certainly where jealousies are, upon every little occasion, ready to rise, it is from the want of love; and so where there is a jealousy of God, there can be no hearty love.

So it is likewise about our listening to accusations. If I do not love such and such and any accuses them to me, I can quickly hearken and entertain any accusation of them. But if I love them, I will not entertain readily any accusations of them. Where there are several parties of men and the bond of love is broken, let there be any accusation against one who is in their way they will not entertain it; but let there come any accusations against men who are of the contrary party, they will readily entertain them. So, if we loved God we would never entertain any ill reports of God. Where the heart stands out against any ill reports of God, certainly the soul loves God exceedingly.

MOTIVE 8. Consider that faith, wherever it is, is first wrought by an almighty power in the soul. Ephesians 1:18–19: "The exceeding greatness of God's power whereby He raised up Christ from the dead" appears in the work of faith. Consider this, if there is such an infinite power of God, the same power that raised Christ from the dead put forth in faith at first, then surely faith is able to do great things. Thus I would reason, that thing that has the choice of God's power, the excellence of the power of God, the thing wherein the glory of God's power appears above all other things, that thing has a great deal of power put into it and is able to do great things. But so it is with faith. Read over all the Book of God and you will never find such expressions of God's power for doing anything that ever He did since the world began as in the first chapter of Ephesians, that has expressions of His power working faith in the soul.

Surely, then, one who has any hope of having the work of God upon him should argue thus: Has God put forth an almighty power in the working of this grace in my soul, and shall this grace be able to do nothing? If this grace in my soul were only able to believe in God so long as I have God in sight, a little power would do this. But my faith is a grace that has a great deal of God's power in it and, therefore, God expects that there must be such things done by it as it may show forth the greatness of His power. If God only gives a man natural gifts, He would have them be improved to the height of them. When God works faith in the soul at first, God says, "I'll put forth a power even beyond whatever I put forth before, above all My works that I have made. When I come to make a believer and to work faith in the soul, there shall be the choice and excellence of My power." When this is done God says to the soul, "O believer, now walk so as to manifest that which is done in your souls, wherein the excellence of My power appears." And by doing so we shall surely walk in a gracious and holy and blessed way by faith in the want of sense.

21

More Motives to Stir Up Weak Believers to Exercise Their Faith When They Want Sense

I shall go on further in some motives for stirring up weak believers in the exercising of their faith.

MOTIVE 9. Surely the sight and sense that we shall come to have after our believing, when there was no sight, will be so much the sweeter and more comfortable. A mercy that comes after God's withdrawing of Himself and our exercising of faith is the sweetest mercy of any mercy; when mercy is raised from the dead, as Isaac, who was born against the apprehension of common sense and was a child of faith. His name was called Isaac, and Isaac signifies laughter, because Isaac was a matter of much joy to his parents. And so certainly whatever child it is that comes of faith is a child of joy. Whatever mercy comes upon the exercise of our faith, and that when all things seem to work contrary, that mercy is a sweet mercy; it will pay for all the afflictions that we had in the time of the want of sense.

MOTIVE 10. They will be stronger against temptations afterwards if in the want of sense and the sight of God's love they can exercise faith. The soul that can do so will be easily able to overcome almost any temptation afterwards. If you can so prevail by faith upon your heart to stand out in such an affliction as this is, when you want the sight and sense of the love of God and yet your faith can work through this, if it can, it will easily be able to overcome any temptation afterwards. Suppose in any other business a man does not have the success he desired and expected, but is crossed in it; it may be that this temptation is very strong upon some, and they begin to be discouraged. But for one who has been acquainted with any spiritual desertions and yet their faith has brought through them, such a one will think, "Surely it is not so much to go on in my way and to work through this discouragement that I had, namely in the want of the sight and sense of God's love. Faith helped me at that dead lift then, and why not now?" And so for any other affliction! Let any affliction be upon their bodies or estates, in respect of their friends, or of any who are near them, those afflictions are nothing in comparison of the want of the sight and sense of God's love in Christ. If the soul is but enabled here to work through this by faith, it will find all afflictions to be but easy to him. Therefore it is of great concern for you to walk by faith in the want of sense.

MOTIVE 11. By this means, if we can exercise faith in the want of sense, we shall turn the greatest afflictions into the greatest blessings. Of all afflictions that are in the world, the want of sight and sense of God's love in Christ is the greatest affliction; but by the exercise of faith we shall make this to be a blessing to us. We shall get an abundance of experience and we shall come to have the love of God more sweet unto us. And then, having gotten through a difficulty as this is, we shall by it come to be more established a great deal more in the constant way of our lives, and come to have more communion with God and delight in God. And so we shall have a blessing by that which is the greatest affliction of all.

MOTIVE 12. Last, consider what a tedious thing it

must be to the Spirit of God for a saint, upon God's withdrawing Himself and the want of sight presently, to have resentful thoughts of God. It would be tedious to any loving husband, if he could never go abroad upon any occasion and be out of the presence of his wife without her presently being jealous; or if in the house he should find fault with any little thing, presently she concludes her husband does not love her because his expressions are not so full, or his countenance so amiable at one time as at another. This would be very grievous to the spirit of a husband to have such a construction to be made. Look how tedious it would be to the spirit of a husband to have such ill constructions made by his carriage or absence upon necessary occasion; so tedious is it to the Spirit of God for a soul to be making such ill constructions when God withdraws Himself, or because He does not always manifest Himself in the same way at one time as He does at another.

Oh, let us take heed that we are not burdensome to the Spirit of God by our unbelief. There are many people who are partly afflicted by melancholy and unbelief, who are very tedious to the spirits of those they converse with; and as they are tedious to the spirits of those with whom they converse, so certainly their carriage is very tedious to the Spirit of God. They grieve the Spirit of God by their unbelief; therefore let us take heed of our unbelief in the want of sense and labor to exercise faith.

OBJECTION. But you will say, "What should we do? It's easy indeed to tell us that we should exercise faith in the want of sight and sense, but it is not so easy to do it."

ANSWER. I confess it is one of the hardest things in the world to exercise faith in the want of sense. Therefore, take the following rules of direction.

# 22

Directions For the Exercise of Faith In the Want of Sense

DIRECTION 1. Be afraid of unbelief as much as you are afraid of presumption. I wish that believers, especially those who are weak, would be as much afraid of unbelief as they are afraid of the sin of presumption. You shall have many who are afraid to presume, but it scarcely enters their thoughts to be afraid of unbelief. If I presume, then, that's dangerous, for I may quickly destroy myself that way. But why should you not be as much afraid to destroy yourself by unbelief? There is not only the destruction in unbelief as well as in presumption, but there is a wronging of the grace of God in it, and so there may be more danger of sin in the one thing as in the other. It's true, there is sin and danger in presumption, and there is sin and danger in unbelief too; and the truth is that unbelief is a more secret sin, and that which we may fall into before we are aware, sooner than the other.

Now if the soul would but reason after this manner: "It's true, I think that the promise of mercy does not belong to me and, therefore I am afraid I should presume. But what if I should wrong the grace of God? Is not that a tender thing? And is there anything in the world that God stands more upon to have honored than His grace in Christ? And what if it should prove that I have wronged the grace of God in Christ all this while? What a sad thing that would be! And would not that be as grievous to God as anything else?"

Oh, if you would but do this it would be a very great help to you, for there would be this use of it: It would make you to be willing to listen as well to those who may further your believing in the grace of God in Christ; that may honor God's grace as much as to listen to those things that may take you off.

We find by experience that those that are weak, let one speak to them never so much by way of encouragement to faith, scarcely listen to what is spoken, or do not remember it; but whatever hints of anything they may have by way of discouraging them, that they mind and their thoughts run after, and work upon all that possibly they can. Now it appears by this that they are not afraid of the sin of unbelief so much as of the sin of presumption. Certainly, next to that sin against the Holy Spirit, there is no greater sin in the world than the sin of unbelief; and it is that which more crosses the designs that God has of honoring Himself than any other sin whatsoever. Therefore, be afraid of it, and charge your heart with it, as you would charge your heart with that which you are most inclined to.

If you were inclined to uncleanness, would not you lay a charge of the least things that way? If you were inclined to worldliness, would not you lay a charge upon your heart against that? So charge your heart to take heed of any beginnings of the sin of unbelief, because that's the sin that you are most inclined to. If you were impatient, would not you be careful to charge your heart to take heed of that sin? Charge your heart to take heed of this sin of unbelief. That's the first rule.

DIRECTION 2. At any time when you have a word that seems to make a case for you, take heed that you do not hearken to anything against that word, but require proof for it out of the Word. For example, if you have anything in God's Word that is presented to you in any way for helping your faith in the want of sense, never listen to anything that makes against that word, but require a proof for it out of the Word. Many times when we have a word that speaks well and encouraging to our faith, we set many times our own fancies, conceits, surmises, jealousies, and fears against the Word, and this does us much harm. When we have a word we should never listen to surmises, nor jealousies and fears, but ask, "Can I have as much out of the Word against me in such a thing as I have in the Word to encourage me in this way? If indeed I can bring out of the Word that they who are thus and thus have no grace, that such and such things as these are, cannot stand with true grace; if I can prove this out of the Word, then it is something."

Where do you have any man or woman who comes with any objections against their estates and conditions, with any of their doubts, who bring any word to strengthen their doubts with? Indeed, the doubts that are in them seem to be very strong and prevail much to discourage their hearts, but is it from the Word that their doubts are strengthened. You shall seldom hear them bring any text of Scripture for their doubts; only they are afraid and feel that never was any of God's people so as they are. But they do not come and say "Sir, here is such a place of Scripture that I read such a day and I think this Scripture makes a case against me." If you would go no further than the Scripture for your doubts, it would be an easy matter to help answer them, for then we could show you what God intends in that Scripture.

But it is almost impossible to give an answer to jealousies and fears; we could answer ten Scriptures sooner than one jealousy and fear that has no ground from Scripture. Give me but a Scripture for your doubts and I can give you another that may be for your encouragement, such as that Scripture where Christ says, "He that cometh unto Me I will in no wise cast off." That Scripture requires nothing but coming to Him. And then, "Ho, everyone that thirsts, come and buy without money and take of the waters of the well of life freely." In these Scriptures we can plainly show you the meaning of the Spirit of God in them for encouragements; but can you show such Scriptures that any of your doubts are grounded upon?

Many of you have many doubts concerning your sanctification, but have you any text that tells you that where sanctification is not perfect, there the soul has no interest in Christ? Therefore this may encourage any soul to come in and believe, because there are no such Scriptures that tell any that because they do not have perfection in their sanctification, or because there are remainders of corruption in them, that therefore they have no interest in God and Christ. If we would take comfort but from Scripture, and we would listen to no objection but from Scripture, then it would be an easy matter to get faith to be exercised and we would walk by faith more than we do, if we would rest upon the Word both for the ground of our encouragement and for our doubting, so as to resolve them, the Word shall be as much the ground of my faith and comforts. Do but hold to this, and then you will be mightily helped to walk by faith and not by sight; for though sight

Directions for the Exercise of Faith

fails us, yet the Word never fails, but abides the same, a sure and everlasting foundation.

DIRECTION 3. If you have any one sign that may encourage you, you may take comfort from that though you do not find another. If upon searching in the Book of God you find any one promise making your case for you, though you may think other things are against you, that one is enough for you to rest your souls upon; for where there is one, though you are not able to apprehend the other, yet there are others too. <u>For that is a certain rule, every promise holds Christ; and where there is any one grace, there's all grace, though it cannot be seen.</u> As a man may know as certainly a wicked man by his living in any one known sin and by his heart closing with it, though he does not live in others, yet there is no sin mortified in that man who has any one sin reigning in him. That is, if he has any one sin that he knows to be a sin, and yet his heart closes with it and is not set against it as an enemy to him, this man has no sin mortified. So, where there is any one grace, there is every grace, though it cannot be seen.

If I should come to one who is carnal, and if I see but one sin of covetousness, of earthliness, of worldliness in him, if I should charge him and say that he is an unclean person too, he would deny it; he thinks himself far from it. Why? Because he does not commit the act of it. But it is certain that where you are under the power of any one sin, there no sin is mortified. So it is where any child of God can but find the work of any one grace. It may be such a one will say, "I can find no work of other graces, but, I bless God, there is some grace I can find. For instance, this grace, that I love the saints, I love the brethren, and I love them because they are God's and upon no other ground; and I find I love the Word, and the more holy the Word is the more I do love it." If there is but this one particular, though you cannot find the exercise of other graces, yet you may certainly conclude that there are all graces. All graces are in that soul where there is any one grace, and this is a mighty help to faith in the want of sense. When you come to examine your heart it may be the devil will be putting you upon those graces that are the weakest of all and are most opposed by your corruptions, and will be ready to tell you that you have *no* grace because you do not have *that* grace. But is there any other grace that you have? If you can find in your souls there is any grace, certainly you may conclude that you have an interest in God and His love, though He is out of sight.

DIRECTION 4. Labor to treasure up some principles, or some certain conclusions and truths that you will stick to, and resolve upon whatever temptations come against them. For instance:

(1) Here is one principle which is as clear as anything in the world, and that I can easily convince any man of who is not in a temptation. But if you are not satisfied in it before a temptation comes, you will not be so soon convinced of it when it has come. This is that one truth: There is no threat in the Word of God that is so absolute that it may not be recalled. Or rather take it thus: There is no certain sign in the Word of God whereby any one can conclude themselves to be a reprobate.

Observe now the difference of God's grace, how God's grace is beyond His wrath and displeasure in this, in the manifestation of it. Promises of mercy you have that are absolute, but as for the threats of God's wrath, you have none but are conditional, yea, and so conditional as they

Directions for the Exercise of Faith

may be recalled again. And you have certain signs of election whereby we may know our election; but signs of reprobation, whereby any man or woman while they live should conclude themselves to be reprobates, there is none in all the Book of God, only that of the sin against the Holy Spirit, which is a sin that such a soul who is making after God and longing after the light of His face is far enough from. Oh, the grace of God there is in this to help against unbelief and help our faith, that God should be pleased to manifest His election to be certain in the Word. "We know your election," said the apostle speaking of the election of others, "for our gospel came to you not in word only, but in power." But there is no certainty of reprobation, for "those whom He hath predestined, them He hath called." We know our predestination by our calling, but we cannot conclude ourselves to be reprobates.

I confess there are some signs that are dangerous ones, that is, such as may make men fear, yea, and conclude too that if they should live and die in such a condition then it is certain they were reprobates. And some are more black brands than others of reprobation, such as turning the grace of God into wantonness; that is one of the blackest brands of reprobation of any; or for God to suffer a man to prosper in a wicked course—but yet these are not certain. Though a soul turns the grace of God into wantonness, yet who knows but that God may convince that soul? Lay this as a principle, that there can be no conclusion of anyone, except that which I touched upon before, no concluding that they are reprobates. And whatever threats there are in the Word, they are not so absolute but there is a way that God propounds in the Word, a way for our souls to deliver themselves from the strength and power of those threats, that is, by believing and by repenting. This is easy for men and women to believe; but in time of temptation it is not so easy to believe this.

Oh, lay this for a conclusion: Let my condition be the worst that possibly can be imagined, let me lay this up for a conclusion: There is no threat that is absolute but the soul while it lives may be delivered from it. And I hear this, that there is no condition so sad that is a certain sign of a reprobate: There can be no conclusions of reprobation as of election.

(2) It is better to set upon things that God requires of us, though we cannot do them as we ought, than to wholly omit them. You will find this an extraordinary help. I know nothing to be a greater hindrance to the work of faith in the soul than this; for those who are enquiring after God and His ways, because they cannot do duties as they ought, or cannot get that good that they desire, therefore think they would be better to let all alone. Temptation works strongly that way, and if temptations can prevail over the heart in this thing, it has yet enough to always keep the soul under the spirit of bondage and unbelief. But if this is a conclusion laid, that I had better be doing what God would have me, and using the means that God requires, than let them alone, it would be better to be doing though I cannot do as I ought.

Sometimes I have said of water that runs through a pipe, though it keeps nothing in, yet it keeps the pipe clean. So though you cannot remember anything of the Word, but it runs through your memory, yet it keeps you from being musty or from gathering filth. You may come to a sermon, and indeed you cannot say that you have gotten much by it, but if you neglect the Word your heart will

Directions for the Exercise of Faith 233

grow a great deal more corrupt than if you come to the Word. And so a man who is sick in his stomach may eat some meat, but his stomach casts it up again. You will say "Would not this man be better to eat no meat at all?" Yet you will give him meat for all that, for there is something that is turned to nourishment that upholds the life of the man. And so it is in the use of the means. Though we think that all the means are lost, yet there is something insensibly that works; and however, you are in the way that God would have you to be in. And if there were nothing else but this, this would be enough. Lay this for a principle and it will be advantageous in the time of desertion.

(3) Where there is no peace with sin, there sin is not a sufficient ground to hinder the peace of the soul. I mean by that, no peace with sin, not only that our consciences are against our sins, but that our hearts, our wills and affections are against them as well as our consciences. I confess the conscience of a wicked man may be against his sin though his sin closes with his will and affections. But where there is a fight against sin by the will and affections, where that soul feels sin to have a contrariety to the disposition of the heart, there is a contrary temper and disposition in the heart to sin. There the remainder of sin is not a sufficient ground to hinder the peace of the soul. There may be a great deal of corruption in the soul, but while it is as a disease and not mingled in the very temperature of the soul, there it is not a sufficient ground to hinder the peace of the soul.

(4) Where the soul finds the want of any grace, or at least is sensible that it cannot be as sensible as it would be, and hunger after that grace, and prizes it above all the comforts in this world, and that for the excellence there is

in it, there the soul cannot conclude against itself that it has no grace in it. It is too much boldness for the soul to conclude against itself that it does not have that grace in it. It is too much boldness for the soul to conclude that God has never wrought such a grace in me if I find that because I do not have the sense of that grace and the work of it as I desire, that this is a burden of my soul, it is that which is the grief of my heart that I lack the exercise of such a grace. And the Lord knows how I would prize it, not only because it is necessary, since I cannot be saved without it, but how I would prize it as that wherein there is an excellence, a beauty, a glory. This is that which my soul longs for, and I am seeking after with all my might. Such a soul cannot conclude that that grace is not wrought within it. Oh, this would answer a hundred doubts, queries, and objections of many people in the time of the affliction of their consciences about grace who will thus conclude, "Well, certainly there's such and such a grace that I do not have, and because I do not have that, I am afraid I have none at all." But if this is put to you, "Is not this the burden of your soul that you want such and such graces as these are, and do you not prize the happy condition of those that have them? And is not your soul in a way of hungering and thirsting after that grace and laboring for it?" You shall speak against the grace and goodness of God to you if you should conclude that you do not have this grace already; it may be in you and under the clods, though, perhaps, you do not see it so clearly in the fruit and effects of it.

(5) There is a faith of adherence where there is not a faith of evidence. Lay up that and take the expression thus: There may be a union with Christ where there is no

Directions for the Exercise of Faith

vision. It is no argument that because I have no vision, therefore I have no union; neither is it an argument that because I have no faith of evidence, therefore I have no faith of adherence. A soul may truly and safely stick and cleave unto God, unto Christ, by a faith of adherence, though it has no faith of evidence to itself for the present. This is helpful to the soul to help it in believing in the want of sense, when God is out of sight. If the soul does not have that faith of evidence that it desires, for it then to conclude it has no faith at all, you may have a faith of adherence, and you should try whether you do not find your heart to cleave to Jesus Christ and to close with Him. Now these principles are to be laid beforehand, and there is no man who is out of temptation but will acknowledge these things.

23

Further Directions for the Exercise of Faith in the Want of Sense

DIRECTION 5. When reasoning and temptations grow strong, the way is not to answer them with reasoning and to seek to satisfy those temptations, but rather to fall to prayer and to spread them before the Lord, as Hezekiah did with Rabshekes' railing letter. The devil comes sometimes and even rails upon God, His truths, His ways, and His saints. But do you go and spread them before the Lord? Do not think to answer reasoning with reasoning; the devil will be too hard. If you begin to reason with flesh and blood, and think to satisfy yourself by your own reasoning, the devil will be too hard; he is too cunning a logician for you. We must not fight with the devil in his way, that is, by reason, for the devil has stronger gifts and reasons than we can have, if we rest on our own understanding.

The way is to fly to Jesus Christ, to beseech Him that He would answer such reasoning and temptations. Oh, let a soul in quietness commit itself to Jesus Christ and spread its case before Him: "Lord, I am at a loss here. I do not know what to say to myself and my condition, only I think that I can say that I love Thee." When Christ spoke to Peter and said, "Lovest thou Me?" He received the reply, "Lord, Thou knowest that I love Thee."

Etch this deep in my heart!

Further Directions for the Exercise of Faith

It may be that temptation comes and says, "If you loved God, you would do thus and thus; and surely these and these things cannot stand with a true love for God." It may be that you cannot answer every particular, but you can go in the quiet of your heart and appeal to God, "Lord Thou knowest that I love Thee. I know not what to say to these things that are suggested; but, Lord, Thou knowest that I love Thee."

Indeed, if a man should come and bring some evidences to you, and reasons to convince you that your heart is worthless and your way are evil, it's not enough for you to stand out and say, "Well, say what you will, yet I believe that my condition is good, and it's not as bad as you make it." It's not for you to answer men so, but when there comea a temptation from the devil you are not bound to give the devil an account, as you are to give your brother an account.

If you go into the presence of God and appeal to God that your ways are right, and that God knows that you love Him, that may be an answer to a thousand temptations that come into your minds. And if you can open your hearts freely in prayer and look up to Jesus Christ, your great Champion, and desire His help to assist you in this combat, this is a better way than to think to stand out with reasoning and wrestling with temptation. Oh, rather, appeal to God in prayer and open your hearts to Him; that's the way. Luther used to say that his prayers were the leeches of his cares. As leeches will suck out corrupt blood, so prayers will get out the strength of temptations. Many physicians in some cases will rather seek to purge the body that way than by giving poison. The leeches sucking out corrupt blood will sooner cleanse the body than poison. And so the leeches of prayer will many times sooner help against a temptation than any other thing that can be done.

DIRECTION 6. In the time of desertion, the direction that we should take is this: Labor to keep in your eye the object of faith so as to behold and look upon that which may help your faith. Set before you the covenant of grace, the freeness and the fullness of God's grace in Christ as it is revealed in the covenant, the plentiful mercy that is there; keep that in your eye. Many, when they want the sight of God's favor, are then altogether poring upon their corruptions, looking upon the black side of the cloud. But though you cannot yet apprehend that God is yours, and the favor and love of God in Christ, yet you may keep in your eye those things that are the object of the faith of such as are true believers. And what is it that raises the faith of believers but presenting the glory and riches of the covenant of grace to them. Now do not turn away your eyes from it.

OBJECTION. You will say, "But I do not know whether it belongs to me or not."

ANSWER. Yet look upon it; keep your eyes upon it, upon some special part of the gospel, some remarkable Scriptures as have most of the gospel in them, such as, "God so loved the world that He sent forth His only begotten Son," and 2 Corinthians 5:19. Such Scriptures that hold forth much of the gospel should be kept in your eyes. Meditate on them; roll them in your thoughts and you do not know what they may work in you.

OBJECTION. You will say, "These things belong to believers."

ANSWER. Nay, they do not belong only to those who are actual believers already; but they are revealed to the end that they might work faith where there is none. They have a generative faculty in them. It is through the gospel that faith is begotten as well as increased. Therefore, keep those things in your eye for the raising of your faith. And that's another help in the want of sense.

DIRECTION 7. I shall give you one more: In the want of sense and sight, let it be your great care, if you think you have not had faith and repentance before, yet now afresh to act on it. That's likewise a rule that upon any occasion in speaking to those in desertions I ever make use of, and shall ever use as a special rule as much as any I know of to help those who are in any spiritual desertions to renew an act of faith and repentance. Yea, if they think they never believed before, yet they should strive to put forth a work of faith and repentance; for it may be the soul has examined and searched to know what the condition is between God and it, and can find no evidence at all that ever it had any grace. Yet what hinders you from believing? Do not spend so much time looking over your old evidences, to find out your evidences that were of ancient date, and forthwith strive to put forth a new act of faith.

If you are at a loss with the temptations of the devil, or your own heart, that you know not what in the world to say, answer thus: "Well, grant the worst that might be, suppose all that has been before was false, yet what hinders me from believing now? Remember what has been said; there is nothing that gives a right to Christ but believing, and nothing gives any man the right to believe but believing, therefore what hinders me that at this instant I may believe?" I do not mean by believing to conclude that my condition is good, for many Christians are held under the spirit of bondage by this. They think the nature of faith is to conclude in their own thoughts that their condition is good, and that they certainly shall be saved. That's the fruit of faith, but not the nature of faith.

The nature of faith is <u>the rolling of the soul upon the free grace of God in Christ</u>. Now though there are many things that may hinder me from concluding that my state is good, yet there is nothing that should hinder me from rolling my soul upon the free grace of God in Christ. A man has some hope that he has such an acquittal or a bond among some papers in his boxes, but he cannot find it; if he has to deal with one who is faithful he may go likely and get his bond renewed, or get an acquittal made anew before he can find his old one. So it is here, we have to deal with a faithful God when many times we have lost our evidences, lost our bonds. The way is to go and renew our acquittals, to renew our bonds, to renew our evidences, that is, to go and exercise faith afresh. What hinders me that now this very morning or evening but that I may put forth an act of faith upon Jesus Christ?

I shall conclude with this one note. I affirmed to you before that there was a faith of adherence where there is not a faith of evidence. Let me now tell you that there is a venturing faith as well as a faith of adherence and evidence. Indeed, this venturing faith is an adherence, but when the soul cannot have encouragement to believe under the notion of adhering to Jesus Christ, it may be the violence of temptation seems to drive it off from adhering. But for the helping of those who are under temptation and want sense altogether, let faith be presented under the notion of venturing. Though we do not have the word

Further Directions for the Exercise of Faith

in Scripture, yet we have the thing itself. Consider that poor woman of Canaan. Though she was put off and called a dog and the like, yet "dogs have crumbs." And we have what was said by Job, "Though He kill me, yet will I trust in Him." And as Esther said, "If I perish, I perish." And so this faith is evident when the soul can but come to this: "Well, it's true, I am out-reasoned by temptation, and I do not know what in the world to say to myself, what my condition is. I see I am puzzled and am never likely to work out this temptation in that way of reasoning I am in. But for my part, I am resolved upon this, if the Lord destroys me He shall destroy me relying upon Him. It's true, I do not know yet whether God will receive me or not. I do not have that evidence, and as for my cleaving to the grace of God in Christ, whether I can do it or not, I cannot tell. But I am resolved on this: Here I will venture and, if I perish, I will perish casting my soul upon the grace of God in Christ. This shall be my way. I am sure if I depart from God I must perish. If I should be weary of God and His ways, and forsake them and embrace my own sinful ways, I am certain that I shall perish there. But I will do this: I will venture my soul here, and here I will lie as a poor, wretched, miserable creature in myself, and I will cast an eye up towards His holy temple, towards the grace of God, and here my soul shall pitch and venture. I'll cast my anchor here. Whether the tempest will be so great that it will break anchor and cable I do not know, but I am sure that if I do not cast anchor, I shall run upon the rocks and split and suffer shipwreck.

I confess that were not the soul in a temptation this would not be enough merely to venture. We must not rest in this; we must still be laboring to find that our souls adhere and cleave to the grace of God in Christ, and never be at peace till we have some assurance of it too. But I declare what is to be done in the time of temptation; when a man is in a storm and tempest, then it is a work acceptable to God, and it has had very often exceedingly good success. When a soul, not knowing what to do, yet at length has concluded thus: "If I am undone I will be undone in Christ's arms, and here I will hang and ride at this anchor; and if the Lord should shake me into hell, yet I'll hang as long as I can and here I'll venture," <u>oh, this will keep you from departing from God, and will be such an acceptable work to God as it's likely that you shall not be long without some manifestation of God to you to encourage you in the way.</u>

And so to make all the former good, I'll leave this one thing with you: Know that all times are not fit times for you to judge of your condition. It's not a fit time to judge whether a tree is alive or dead in the midst of winter. It is not a fit time to judge the constitution of the body in the fit of a fever, or of the comeliness of one's countenance in the time of a fever. No, if you would judge the body, you must do it when it is in health; and so if you would weigh gold, it must be when the scales may stand even. There are many poor, weak believers who never passed any judgement upon themselves but in the hour of a temptation, which is the most unfit time. No, rather wait until you are yourself again, and then you may be more fit to judge your estate.

These directions may be some good help for your faith in the want of sense so that, while God withdraws Himself, yet you may be able in some measure through the Lord's assistance to walk by faith when you cannot walk by sight.

24

Helps to Walk by Faith When God Appears as an Enemy to the Soul

The principal thing in a saint's walk with God is to walk by faith. Observe but this rule in all duties that you do perform; let it be your main care to activate faith in all duty; it is that which believers are faulty in. They make conscience of such and such duties, and they are careful not only to do those things that God requires, but to do them in the manner that God requires, that is, in sincerity, in zeal, in strong affection and seriousness. Yet they do not so much consider the acting of faith. The principal ingredient in every duty is the acting of faith. If we pray, it is the prayer of faith; if we hear, it is mixing the Word with faith; if we receive the Lord's Supper, it is the discerning of the Lord's body. In every service we must look how much faith has been exercised. If you perform any duty, look back: "I have done what God requires of me, but how have I done it? How has my soul closed with the free grace of God in Christ after I have done all that I can? Yet have I been beat down in mine own thoughts and advanced free grace? Have I found my soul acting upon the promise at this time when I have been praying and hearing and receiving?" These thoughts are seldom in the hearts of many Christians. They look rather at the performing of a duty in a moral way than in a true Christian and evangelical way.

I shall proceed to some further cases about walking by faith, and they may be referred to in these two headings: First, either how a Christian should walk by faith in the time of affliction, or, second, how he should walk by faith when God calls him to any difficult service.

When God lays any affliction upon us, yet it is not sense that we give way to, but it is faith that we act on in our affliction.

And then when God calls me to any work, though at first I may think it is beyond me and I shall never be able to accomplish it, yet in this difficult work I am to walk by faith, to act out faith; and if any thing will carry me through, it is faith.

First, for afflictions, they are of two sorts, either inward or outward afflictions, which we have treated already. The want of the sight of God is a great inward affliction, and we might bring it under this heading. Yet there are some inward afflictions that are beyond this. Not only that God withdraws Himself from the soul and there is the want of sight, but what if God comes against the soul as an enemy? That is beyond God's withdrawing Himself, so that there is no sight of Him. And yet even then a saint should walk by faith. Not only when God is withdrawn, but when God shall appear as an enemy; for many souls are ready to say, "The Lord has done this to me." So to help for when God appears as an enemy to the soul:

1. Here is help, so that you may not despond and faith may not be shattered. This is not such a condition but other dear saints of God have been put into heretofore. It is some encouragement for the act of faith when I know that my condition is not such but that others of the dearest saints of God have been in that condition—and yet in

Helps to Faith When God Appears As an Enemy

that condition they walked by faith and so got out of it. In Job 13:24, see what the complaint of that holy man was: "Wherefore hidest Thou Thy face, and holdest me for Thine enemy?" Here you have the want of sight, yea, here is a degree even beyond that: "Thou hidest Thy face and holdest me as an enemy." God appeared so against him, even as an enemy. It was not in regard of his outward afflictions and losses that he looked at so much, but in regard of spiritual afflictions that were upon his soul. God tore and rended him even as an enemy, and so it has been with many others of God's servants, such as Heman in Psalm 88. If read that psalm you shall find that surely it was no less that God appeared to him but as an enemy.

2. But for your further help, know that it may be that these are but the dark apprehensions of unbelief, and not indeed that God really is as an enemy to you. It was certainly the unbelief of the people of Israel that caused them to say, when they were brought into difficulties, "God has brought us into the wilderness because he HATED us," presently concluding that God was an enemy because they did not have what they wanted. And that's the vain, froward disposition of some. If they cannot have what they would have, it is because God hates them. This is the unbelief you are to check yourself for.

3. But suppose there was a reality in it, that God appeared indeed as an enemy. Certainly the best way is not to fly from Him. Though He has the sword of justice in His hand ready to strike you, yet the best way is to come and crouch before Him, to lie down in His presence, to put your neck even to the stroke of justice, and to exercise a venturing faith. However, do not fly from Him though

He appears as an enemy, for nothing can be gained by flying from Him.

4. Yea, if your soul is at enmity with sin, certainly God is not your enemy, whatever He appears to you to be. Though He seems to come in never such a terrible manner against you, yet look into your heart and see whether there are—not only in your conscience, but in your heart—contrary principles unto it. God is never an enemy to that soul that is an enemy to sin.

5. And yet further, suppose there was a reality that God was an enemy. Yet know there is enough in Christ to reconcile enemies. Romans 5:10: "For if when we were enemies we were reconciled to God." Even when we were enemies; therefore, though you are an enemy and God appears to you as an enemy, yet when we were enemies we were reconciled to God. You may then act in faith upon the purchase of the blood of Christ, though you apprehend yourself as an enemy, and God coming as an enemy against you.

6. It may be it is because your heart is loose and careless and negligent in your way that therefore God seems to come against you as an enemy, as He did in a terrible manner against Moses. You know the Lord came in a terrible manner against Moses to stop him in the inn; surely then He came in the appearance of an enemy, but it was because Moses had been negligent of the circumcising of the child. You are to search and examine your way; what negligence, looseness, wantonness, and deadness is in your heart? What sluggishness is in your heart? Why, God only draws His sword to awaken you and to stir you up. Do as those whom Joab came against: "Send the head of

Shimei the son of Bicri and we are gone." So renounce sin and God will appear no more as an enemy.

7. Still, let God's appearance be never so terrible, it's fitting for you to trust in Him and say with Job: "Though He kills me, yet will I trust Him." Suppose He does intend to destroy me, yet if I am destroyed, I will trust with my heart pursuing Him. My heart shall rely upon Him even while He is striking the fatal blow upon me. Faith is able to see love through frowns. Though God seemed to be never so angry with David, yet he could say, "Cast me not out of Thy presence." It is a speech of Luther, speaking in the commendations of faith, that it's one great commendation for a man to love God when God shows himself an enemy. And that is the excellence of faith, to enable the soul to do that.

These meditations may be of some help to the exercise of faith and walking by it in such a condition.

OBJECTION. But God lets Satan out upon me in great and sore and strong temptations. And would He let out the devil upon me so as He does if He loved me? Shall I be able to walk by faith when I am hurried by the temptations of the devil?

ANSWER. That is a sore and a great affliction that the saints endure. As for that, still you must know that it has been the portion of the dear saints of God to have Satan let out upon them too. We shall find that God said to Satan that He had given Job into his hand. Satan was let out upon him, and that in a fearful manner. We read in Luke of a daughter of Abraham who had been bound by Satan for eighteen years. Satan prevails many times very much upon the dear children of God. Paul had a prick in the flesh, a messenger of Satan who was sent to buffet him.

And Luther often complained of the most horrid temptations of Satan, and made all the outward afflictions that he endured, the enmity and rage of all the Popish party, to be nothing compared to those inward afflictions that he had in his spirit. I remember that upon it he said that there are three things make a divine—reading, meditation, and temptation. In meditation he included prayer, which the Scripture calls meditation of the heart. These make a divine, and God prepared him for great services that He intended for him by his temptations upon him.

25

Encouragement For a Saint When God Lets the Devil Out Upon Him

Know therefore further for the help of your faith, do not let your heart despond. Though the Lord lets out the devil upon you, yet walk by faith in that condition, for:

1. At such a time when you were not apprehensive or sensible of Satan, then you did not have those horrid temptations that now you have, yet he had more power over you then than now. And therefore you have no cause to be discouraged in this.

2. Lay this up as a help to your faith: God has very good ends why He exercises His dearest servants even with such a heavy affliction as this is, the strong temptations of Satan. Satan in this case is like the shepherd's dog. The shepherd sets his dog to worry the sheep a little, but it is to bring the sheep in and not to kill them, for he calls it off when he pleases. So Satan is, as it were, the dog that God, the great Shepherd, sends sometimes to worry the sheep, but so as He calls him off when He pleases. It is but to bring those who are wandering into the fold. And as tempests and storms clear the air, even so hideous and terrible temptations will clear the soul; the soul comes to clear up after them; you come to know your hearts a great deal better than before.

3. Further, know that Christ Himself was tempted. If you read the story of Christ's temptations in Matthew 4, it

is a story of excellent use, and a mighty encouragement for the exercise of faith in the time of temptation. Even the Lord Jesus Christ, the Son of God did not escape it. Indeed, the devil had so much power even to carry His body up and down and to set it upon the pinnacle of the temple and tempt Him to as hideous things as you are tempted to. He tempted Him even to the greatest idolatry that ever was, to fall down and worship him; to the most fearful blasphemy, to cast off God as His Father and to acknowledge even the devil himself to be a god unto Him. All these were from these two ends, either:

First, that Christ might be a merciful High-Priest, one who might be sensible of your temptations, He being tempted Himself. Christ knows what it is to be tempted by the devil, therefore we read in Hebrews 4:13: "We have not a High-Priest which cannot be touched with the feelings of our infirmities, but was in all points tempted like as we are, yet without sin." It's true, the temptation did not prevail in Him to sin, yet He was tempted likewise in all things. There is no temptation more hideous and blasphemous that Satan tempts us with than he tempted Christ Himself; and this was that He might a merciful High-Priest, and that He might be touched with our infirmities.

Second, yes, and not only so, but you are to look upon the temptations of Satan as part of Christ's humiliation, part of His sufferings that is meritorious, as that which takes out the sting and evil of temptations. The venom of the temptation is taken out by Christ's subjecting Himself unto death; so the sting and venom of temptations is taken by Christ's subjecting Himself unto them.

4. Yet further, we find that Christ prays for His people that they may not be overcome with temptations. You must walk by faith in the time of temptation, that is, not only act your faith upon Christ's temptations, to take out the sting and venom of it, but act your faith upon Christ's prayer. That prayer that Christ prayed for Peter, surely He made it for you too; you may as well apply that prayer for Peter as Paul in Hebrews applied the promise that was made for Joshua. In Luke 22:31-32, Christ told Peter that Satan had desired to winnow him as wheat; but Christ prayed that his faith might not fail. And observe, the main thing that is to be exercised in the time of temptation is faith, and if faith does not fail the soul is well enough; and Christ prays for this. Now you know what Christ said, that His Father always hears Him. In time of temptation it's best to pray much rather than to reason with temptations, and make use of the prayer of Jesus Christ. "Oh, blessed God, did not Thy Son, when He was in the days of His flesh, pray for one of His members, that when Satan would sift and winnow him that his faith might not fail. Oh, Lord, let me have the fruit and benefit of this prayer. This is that which I act my faith upon."

Again, stirring up faith is the special help against temptations. In 1 Peter 5:9, you shall see there that the way against temptations is not for the soul to sink down in a sullen and discontented way, to have horror and trouble overwhelm it, but to stir up an act of faith. In verse 8, he says, "That our adversary, the devil, like a roaring lion walketh about, seeking whom he might devour." Then in verse 9 comes the injunction: "whom resist STEADFAST in the faith." It is the work of faith that is the great help in resisting the strength of temptation; it is not so much to stand reasoning the case. "Oh, this temptation is a hideous thing and I hope I shall never yield unto it." No, but exercise faith, and this shield of faith will quench the fiery darts of the devil (Ephesians 6:16). Faith is not only a shield to keep off the fiery darts, but to quench them.

5. Besides, know for the help of your faith in time of temptation that Christ has broken the serpent's head already. He has broken it for you according to the promise: "The seed of the woman shall break the serpent's head." The serpent can nibble at your heel, but his head is broken; his strength is over-powered. And the conquest that Christ has over the devil we find set out in Colossians 2:14–15 and Hebrews 2:14–15. In Colossians 2 it says: "And having spoiled principalities and powers, He made a show of them openly, triumphing over them in it." That is, in His cross, He has spoiled principalities and powers. By principalities and powers must be meant the angels of darkness, the devils. These He has spoiled when He was upon the cross. He took their power and spoiled them and triumphed over them. This was so that they would never be able to mischief His saints' walk by faith in temptations by exercising faith upon this expression of Christ.

And the other Scripture is from Hebrews 2: "For as much then as the children are partakers of flesh and blood, He also Himself likewise took part of the same, that through death He might destroy him that hath the power of death, that is, the devil, and deliver them who through fear of death were all their life time subject to bondage." Here is a most sweet and excellent Scripture to exercise faith upon in time of temptation. Christ through death has destroyed him who has the power of death, that is, the devil. The devil comes with hideous temptations and tells you that you shall die and perish and makes you apprehend death in a very terrible manner. Christ has destroyed him, to deliver you who, through fear of death, were all your life subject to bondage. It may be that through the strength of temptation all your days you have been in bondage. Now this was one end why Christ died, that He might destroy the devil who has so much power in death to afflict the soul with the dreadful apprehensions of it.

6. Then likewise know that there are many excellent and sweet promises that we have in Scripture that temptations shall not prevail. And the way to help against that is to turn to those Scriptures and to work your faith upon them. I will name some. 1 Corinthians 10:13: "There hath no temptation taken you but such as is common to men; but God is faithful, who will not suffer you to be tempted above that you are able, but will with the temptation also make a way of escape that ye may be able to bear it." Here is as full an expression as our hearts can desire. God will not allow us to be tempted above our strength, but will with the temptation also make a way to escape. Plead this promise; challenge this promise in the time of temptation, and this is the way to be delivered from the strength of temptation.

Romans 16:20: "The God of peace shall tread down Satan under your feet shortly." "The God of peace." Observe, it is not only a promise that Satan shall be trodden down, but God shall tread him down as a God of peace. And mark the issue of the acting of faith upon such promises as these. In Romans 8:38–39, you know what the triumph of the apostle was, that he was "persuaded that neither death, nor life, nor angels, nor principalities, nor powers, nor things present, nor things to come, nor height, nor depth, nor any other creature" should ever separate him from the love of God, nor the chief of all the devils—and his soul triumphs in this.

7. Be sure to remember this rule: If you think to overcome temptations by reasoning, the devil will be too hard for you, for he is the old serpent, very full of skill, knowledge, and experience that he has had these six thousand years. Oh, there are wiles of Satan and depths of Satan! He has more natural strength in understanding, and a deeper reach in things, than all the men in the world have. Though he is fallen, yet he has not lost all the natural understanding that he had when God made him; and therefore you, being a poor, weak believer, are not able to stand against him by reasoning, any more than against the most cunning cheater who ever lived in the world.

8. Yea, let me tell you by way of encouragement for the acting of your faith in the time of temptation that it is not such a heavy condition for the Lord to let the devil out upon one in the strongest and most terrible temptation as for the devil to have power to draw to any sin. Or the power of sin that God leaves any man unto is a greater evil than the strongest temptation that ever befell any in the world; for the devil, though he is strong, yet is not able to force any man to sin. To be given up therefore to the power of any one sin is a heaver judgement than to be given up to the strongest temptation of the devil.

OBJECTION. But you will say, "It may be that is my case. I think I feel corruption to be exceedingly strong in me."

ANSWER. Look at the opposition of your soul, when it is not only your conscience, but your will and affections against sin. Corruptions stir in you, but you can appeal to

God not only because conscience puts you upon it, but you find your very heart, will, and affections opposing this. This is a greater good than the other is an evil, and therefore you should not be discouraged.

Again, walk by faith even in the stirrings of corruption, for the Lord has made a gracious promise that sin shall not have dominion over you in Romans 6:14. Oh, plead that promise with God; put that bond in suit and act your faith upon that promise. "O Lord, sin stirs forth in me and I am afraid lest it should prevail. But, Lord, have you not said that it shall not have dominion over me?"

9. Further, for the help of your faith, even in the time of the stirrings of corruption, take that Scripture in Romans 5:6, where the Lord is said to be merciful even to the ungodly in a way of justification, for so He speaks of that: "For when we were without strength, in due time Christ died for the ungodly." Though there is much ungodliness, yet Christ is propounded as dying for the ungodly. Therefore if one who is ungodly can exercise faith upon the death of Christ, I mean, has seen much ungodliness prevailing in him, but now can act out faith upon such a promise as that is, that Christ died for the ungodly, there may be a walking by faith though there is much corruption prevailing.

And know that you have to deal with God in the way of a covenant of grace. There may be many imperfections, and much corruption may stand with the covenant of grace. Though it's true, to live under the power of any known sin cannot stand with the covenant, yet much stirrings of corruptions and many times prevailing of corruptions may stand with the covenant. We know if a usurper comes and seeks to have dominion over a country that does not belong to him, so long as there is enough opposition that he cannot get upon the throne to make laws and to cause the men to lay down their weapons, he has no dominion there. But when he gets power so as to sit on the throne, and men cast down their weapons and come and submit to his laws, he has dominion. And so sin shall never have dominion over the saints.

Last, exercise your faith even in this case upon the attributes of God, as I hinted at in general when I treated exercising faith when God is out of sight. So when corruption prevails, look up to God as a gracious God who is merciful and pitiful towards His poor, sick children. Suppose that you had a child who had gotten into an inner room and had shut the door, and there was wringing his hands and making his moan that he could love his father and mother no more. Oh, then how would your bowels yearn towards him, though indeed there was much untowardness in the child. "I have heard Ephraim bemoaning himself," said God. If you, when you are alone, bemoan yourself that you have such a disobedient heart that you can love and fear and obey God no more, surely you have to deal with a Father who will spare His child as a father spares his only son that serves him. Therefore walk by faith not withstanding such corruptions that greatly trouble you and many times prevail upon you.

26

Saints Must Walk by Faith In Times of Affliction

OBJECTION. But God follows me with lamentable and sore afflictions together with my sin. What should I do in that case?

ANSWER. You must walk by faith here. This likewise befell Paul. He was troubled with temptations and stirrings of corruption, and cried out sometimes that he was sold under sin and many great and sore afflictions were upon him. But through the exercise of faith he was able to go on in his way and to walk with God in the midst of the greatest and sorest afflictions that befell him. This is a point of very great use to show how faith acts in afflictions and how the soul may be able to walk with God comfortably in the time of afflictions. The use of faith is great in time of affliction. Hope that has all its strength from faith is called an anchor, a helmet and shield. Now the use of these things is in time of storms, in time of danger and opposition. Then (if ever) faith will show what it is able to do, as David said to the King of Achish, "Thou shall know what thy servant is able to do." And so when God calls to an affliction, God calls to faith, "Come, let's see what you are able to do." Now faith helps in time of affliction in many ways.

1. The first and principal help of faith in affliction, whereby a saint is able to walk, is by looking upon God. It

is God in Christ who is the proper object for the eye of faith to look upon. You know from Hebrews 11 that Moses was willing to endure affliction with the people of God, but how? He saw Him who was invisible; he endured; he went on in a constant way of suffering afflictions, but it was by the sight of that God who was invisible. Now the eye of faith, by pitching itself upon God, mightily carries the heart through the afflictions.

For example, it sees in afflictions the love of God. In Hebrews 12:6 we read that God chastises whom He loves. But how can this be seen but by faith? When God chastises me yet He loves me; and how easy is it for the soul to walk with God in afflictions when he can see the love in the rod? And so in Revelation 3:19 we have the love of God in afflictions.

2. There is the wisdom of God in afflictions. He works wisely in afflictions. The Lord considers what affliction is, and He measures out afflictions suitable unto the conditions of the servants who are in affliction. You have a most excellent Scripture for that in Psalm 31:7, where the psalmist says, "I will be glad and rejoice in Thy mercy, for Thou hast considered my trouble. Thou hast known my soul in adversities." "Thou hast considered my trouble." A man who is impatient under trouble considers his trouble with all its circumstances and arguments; but you shall not need to consider your trouble, to be so poring over your trouble, for God Himself considers your trouble. He considers what a proportion there is in the trouble to your strength; the Lord considers the kind of trouble; the Lord considers the degree of the trouble, the measure of it and the continuance of it. There's nothing to be considered in any trouble but God considers it. Oh, it's a great help to a

soul to walk by faith to consider this: "There is nothing in my affliction that is to be considered but Thou, O Lord, consider it first."

3. Then also the soul looks upon God's faithfulness in afflictions in Psalm 119:75: "In very faithfulness Thou hast afflicted me." There is faithfulness in this as well as in fulfilling promises; and you know that faithfulness is a special object for faith.

4. The soul looks upon God's tenderness in the time of affliction. How compassionate and sensible God is of my afflictions, as in Isaiah 63:9: "In all their afflictions He was afflicted." He was afflicted Himself. He was sensible of all those afflictions. He sympathized with them in the furnace.

5. Again, the soul looks upon God's protection in afflictions and so exercises faith. It is a notable Scripture in Psalm 57:1: "Thou wilt hide me under the shadow of Thy wings until these calamities be overpast." His afflictions were very grievous and sad, but mark how he exercised faith: He looked upon himself as under the shadow of God's wings.

6. Further, faith takes hold of the strength of God in afflictions and so comes to have strength to bear afflictions beyond all natural strength. Isaiah 27 is a most famous Scripture for the way of the soul in exercising faith in the time of affliction: "Or let him take hold of my strength that he may make peace with me; and he shall make peace with me." The Lord there was speaking of His church as a vine in the beginning of the chapter. Now as a vine has little strings that God has, in the work of nature, put into it for to catch hold upon anything that is next to it to under-prop it; because the vine is a weak creature in

itself, therefore God supplies the want of strength by those little strings. So, He says, "Let him take hold of My strength; let him by faith, when storms and tempests, when afflictions come, let him take hold of My strength." As the vine in time of a storm, if it can catch hold upon any strong thing to support it, the vine keeps up, whereas otherwise it falls upon the ground. So if there is faith to take hold of the strength of God in the time of affliction, then the soul is supported and enabled to go through the affliction.

7. Yet further, faith not only takes hold of God's strength, but that's one remarkable thing, faith looks upon God as making it the greatest thing that He delights and glories in, namely to help His servants in time of affliction. In Isaiah 25:4, you shall find the prophet setting God out in His glory, and it is in the helping of His people out of their afflictions. So also in Isaiah 30:18, the Lord waits to be gracious, as a work that His heart is most set upon. Then in the latter end of Micah 7 we read: "Who is a God like unto Thee, pardoning iniquity, transgression and sin?" And so He goes on in showing His pity and compassion towards His servants. "Who is a God like unto Thee, and that in this thing, in the way of mercy?" God when He would show His glory to Moses, showed the glory of the attributes of His goodness and mercy. Now when faith can look upon God, God is not only able and willing, but accounts it His great glory. The great masterpiece of all His works is to be helpful to His poor servants in the days of their troubles and afflictions. Upon this the soul walks by faith.

27

More Ways Faith Helps the Soul In Times of Affliction

8. Another thing wherein faith helps the soul is this: Faith takes away the guilt of sin, and so makes the affliction easy to be borne. It takes away the guiltiness, and so it comes to purify the heart; guiltiness makes affections very heavy and sad. When Joseph's brethren had guilt upon their consciences, it made the affliction to sting indeed (Genesis 42:21). That place in Romans 5:1 is notable for this: "We being justified by faith, have peace with God." And what then? "We rejoice in tribulations." We can easily rejoice in tribulations if we are justified by faith and so have peace with God. It is the guilt of sin that is the sting in afflictions. Luther said, "Strike, Lord, strike, for I am absolved from my sin." Let God take away guilt and it's an easy matter to bear afflictions. And this is the proper work of faith, to justify the soul before the Lord and to take away the curse of afflictions.

All the sting and curse of an affliction comes by sin; it comes by the law. Faith acts upon the afflictions of Christ, upon what Christ has suffered, and so comes to take away the sting of all afflictions. "O death where is thy sting?" Thanks be to God through Jesus Christ. It's all taken away in the Lord Jesus Christ; and so faith comes to turn afflictions into good, our water into wine.

9. Afflictions that were evil before come to be turned into good, as when Moses took up the serpent. It was a serpent before he touched it, but when he took it up it was a rod in his hand and of use to him. So though afflictions in themselves are as a serpent ready to devour, yet, being touched by the hand of faith, they are a rod, and such a rod as is useful. They are turned into good, and this is a work of faith, to make such a strange kind of alteration in afflictions. There is a notable Scripture in Job 5:19 concerning afflictions: "He shall deliver thee in six troubles, yea, in seven there shall no evil touch thee." It's a very strange expression. Though you are under many troubles, no evil shall touch you; the evil is taken away; the sting is gone though the trouble is there. If the sting is taken out of a bee, though it may make a buzzing so as to scare a child, yet a man of understanding is not afraid.

10. Again, faith enables the soul to look upon the issue of afflictions as present, and to conclude deliverance out of afflictions; though they are not actual, yet faith makes them as if they were actual and real. Hosea 6:2: "After three days He will revive." He will revive. Though He has smitten us, yet we can look upon our reviving as a certain thing. "After three days, He will revive us." And in Job 23:10: "I shall come forth as gold." I know what the issue of all will be, it will be good; and this is as if it were present to the soul. The soul by faith sees the quiet fruit of righteousness that will come of all afflictions. How easy it is to walk by faith in afflictions when I can see the issue of all as present and good coming out of all afflictions.

11. Faith helps in afflictions by resting upon the Word. In Psalm 119:49-50 David tells you what it was that supported him in the time of his affliction, namely the Word.

This is the way that a believer helps himself in afflictions. He does not so much fly to this duty or the other duty, and fall a whining and crying out and wringing his hands, showing passion and distemper; but he goes and turns over the Word, and if he finds the Word speaking well unto him, that's what supports the soul in the time of trouble. When God says, "I will be with you in six troubles and in seven, and in the fire and in the water, they shall do you no hurt," faith rests upon these things.

The promises that God has made to help the soul in afflictions are many. Take one Scripture, Isaiah 27:7–8, "Hath he smitten him as he smote those that smote him? Or is he slain according to the slaughter of them that are slain by him? In measure, when it shooteth forth, thou wilt debate with it. He stayeth his rough wind in the day of the east wind." It's as sweet and excellent a Scripture for faith to rest upon as almost any I know. The day of the east wind is a day of great trouble and danger, a cold and nipping wind; but God stays His rough wind. He pities them, and in measure He will consider; they are as young tender buds, and God sees that they were not able to bear it, and therefore God deals with them according to their tenderness. Oh, that you would consider this, you who think your afflictions are great. Every man and woman is ready to think their affliction to be the greatest. It is an east wind that is upon you, but there might have come a rough wind in the day of the east wind, but God stays that, because in measure He would debate with you, as in Psalm 103:13–14.

12. Besides, in afflictions faith exercises thus. It makes up all in God: "Such and such creature comforts are taken from me, but faith is such an excellent principle that it

makes up all in God." This is as great an excellence of faith as any, and those who are believers know what the meaning of this is. This, I confess, is a riddle to many, to make up their losses in God. "Such a heavy affliction has befallen me, but when the soul can go and make up all in God, here's the work of faith, to close with God. The Lord is an all-sufficient good, and what I had before in the creature was but as in the pipe or conduit; but I have the fountain now in having God. This is the principal work of faith.

"I thirst for Thee," said David, "in a dry land"—not for water, but for Thee, for Thou canst make up the want of water." This is the very nature of grace. What is the very chief work of faith but this, the giving up of itself wholly to God as the all-sufficient good, as the infinite all-sufficient good, and to be satisfied in Him alone, whatever I want in any creature? This is the very primary act of faith, and the excellence of faith appears in this. And therefore it's very useful in the day of Jacob's trouble.

28

Exhortation to Exercise Faith In the Evil Day

I shall draw all to a close about this point for the present, and that is to labor with you to exercise faith in the evil day, to walk by faith when the clouds are over you. Do you think that faith is of no other use than a sundial, only good in times of fair weather? Surely it is not so with faith to be of use only on a sunshine day; but it is of use especially in stormy winter weather. Take this one note from that Scripture you have in 1 Peter 1:5, that all the power that there is in God will not help you any further, or you cannot expect help from all the power there is in God any further than there is an exercise of faith: "Who are kept," said the apostle, "by the mighty power of God." But how? "Through faith unto salvation." We are kept by the power of God, but through faith. It's not enough for you to say that there is an infinite and glorious God who has all power and excellence in Him, for there is none of this power that will be let out to you but through faith; it must be through an act of faith. Oh, what God has laid upon this grace of faith, that though He has so much power to help the creature, yet He says all power shall wait upon the exercise of faith. "I will wait till I see faith being put forth before I will put forth power in any extremity."

You know what Christ said, "He could not do any great work because of their unbelief." Why, blessed Savior, is Thy power lessened that Thou canst not do any great work? It is because of unbelief. Unbelief comes and stops, as it were, the arms of an infinite power. You are a poor, weak creature and are afraid that you shall fall off. Oh, how shall I be kept through all the trials and dangers and discouragements I meet with in my wilderness travels? God is able to do it, but how shall you have the use of this power? It must be through faith. Oh, the necessity that there is of faith then in an afflicted condition. And this exercise of faith will mightily quiet the soul in the time of affliction.

In Psalm 62 you have an excellent Scripture for quieting your hearts in the days of affliction by the exercise of faith: "My soul, wait upon God." It may be read according to the original thus: "My soul, keep silent to God, for my expectation is from Him." By the exercise of faith the soul is silent. But what I would further note from this Scripture is this. It may be you will say, "I have endeavored to put forth an act of faith in the time of affliction, and yet for all that I do not find my heart quiet." Though you have endeavored once, yet do it again! You shall observe how the soul gets ground by the exercise of faith in the time of affliction if you compare the beginning of Psalm 62 with the middle: "Truly my soul waiteth upon God, from Him cometh my salvation. He only is my rock and my salvation. He is my defense, I shall not be greatly moved" (verses 1–2). At first he was only able to say, "He is my defense and my rock, I shall not be greatly moved." But remember after he had been exercising faith, he had a higher expectation than before: "He only is my rock and my salvation. He is my defense, I shall not be moved." Now I am fixed. Whatever storms and troubles come, I am in a safe condition. I shall not be moved at all.

Oh, that you would but lay up these things so that you may have faith in readiness whenever it should come to act. As that place in the Psalms that speaks of David in the trouble of his spirit, he said that at what time he was afraid, he would trust in God. Not only that David was afraid, but at what time he was afraid he would trust in God. So against what time you are afflicted, you should lay up these things so that you may have use of them, as Mary hid Christ's sayings in her heart. At the time when you are afflicted, the time when temptation comes, the time when God hides Himself, the time when God appears as an enemy, know that God calls you to the exercise of this glorious grace of faith, which is "the substance of things hoped for, the evidence of things not seen," as the apostle describes it. Thus you may walk with God by faith here on earth and hereafter enjoy Him by sight in heaven, where we shall know Him as we are known and behold Him face to face and shall see Him as He is, so far as creatures are capable of that blissful, beatific vision in the great day of revelation of Jesus Christ, the only King of saints.

Finis

Other Titles from The Northampton Press

Sermons on the Lord's Supper, by Jonathan Edwards. Contains 15 sermons by the great New England preacher, 13 of which were previously unpublished. 272 pages HB

Sermons on Important Doctrines, by John Colquhoun. A great Scottish preachers deals with justification, sanctification, salvation from sin, Christ as our righteousness, and others. 252 pages HB.

The Christian Father's Present to His Children, by John Angell James. This book shows that the best gift any father can leave his children is a godly upbringing. 326 pages HB

Heaven Taken by Storm, by Thomas Watson. Watson shows the "holy violence" that is necessary to storm the gates of heaven. 148 pages HB

Saving Faith, by John Colquhoun. This book distinguishes true faith from its counterfeits. 300 pages HB

Light and Heat: The Puritan View of the Pulpit, by Dr. R. Bruce Bickel. The best book on Puritan preaching in print today. 180 pages HB

The Christian on the Mount, by Thomas Watson. This is a Puritan treatise on the art of meditation. 132 pages HB

Distinguishing Traits of Christian Character, by Gardiner Spring. What marks a man as a true child of God? Which ones cannot be counterfeited? 150 pages, HB

Studies on Saving Faith, by Arthur Pink. This is a hard-hitting rebuttal to the "easy-believism" that is so prevalent in our day. It shows that repentance is necessary for salvation. 217 pages, HB

A Dialogue Between a Catholic Priest and a Protestant, by Matthew Poole. A debate over the issues dividing these two very different faiths. 145 pages, HB.

The Precious Things of God, by Octavius Winslow. A warm devotional book that lists those things that God finds precious. 280 pages, HB.

Sighs From Hell, by John Bunyan. The author of *Pilgrim's Progress* was also a fine Bible expositor. This is his treatment of Luke 16, a story Christ told of Dives and Lazarus. It is especially timely in light of a popular mega-church pastor's book denying a literal hell. 168 pp. HB

Preparing For Eternity, by Mike Gendron. The author was a devout Roman Catholic for 34 years before God opened his eyes to biblical and doctrinal truth. In this book he compares Roman Catholic dogma with Scripture truth. Topics such as the proper role of Mary, the ultimate source of authority, the mass, purgatory, the sufficiency of Christ's sacrifice, and others are examined. 250 pp, PB.